Building Biology
Criteria and
Architectural Design

Building Biology
Criteria and Architectural Design

Nurgül Ece

Birkhäuser
Basel

Contents

Foreword

Just as many animals build nests and sometimes
even decorate them, humans also like to
be actively engaged in the design and creation
of their living environment.

"I would like to write a book about architecture based on the principles of building biology and to show that it is possible to design and build structures that are not only contemporary and modern, but at the same time healthy and sustainable," Nurgül Ece—architect, Building Biology Consultant IBN, and author of this book—told me over the phone when asking for my support with this project. I agreed right away and was excited, especially as this book was to showcase real-life exemplary projects, and many designers and clients had been calling for precisely such a publication. Together we selected suitable projects and contacted the designers, skilled craftspeople, and building owners involved.

What constitutes a building biology-based building? The primary focus is on the occupants: their health and their needs. Furthermore, the environment, which forms the basis of our existence, has to be protected as best as possible. And such a building, of course, should also meet economic and functional requirements.

In my opinion, the desire to build is a basic human need in the same way as eating, drinking, and sleeping are. Just as many animals build nests and sometimes even decorate them, humans also like to be actively engaged in the design and creation of their living environment. Children still respond to this fundamental need. As far as they are allowed and given the opportunity, they will build all kinds of structures with passion—big and small—using chairs, tables, blankets, rocks, branches, grass, paints, and ultimately anything that is somehow appropriate. Some adults have maintained this passion, sometimes con-

sciously choosing a creative job to work, for example, as craftspeople, artists, or architects.

People who have the opportunity of living or working in a building based on the principles of building biology—whether they are the homeowners, tenants, or professionals—can consider themselves very lucky. The passion and pleasure of being actively and creatively involved in the design, building, and crafting process, the careful selection of building materials, furniture, and furnishings, as well as the creation of a good indoor climate and sophisticated building systems, all of these make for a happy, healthy, and sustainable living and work environment. There is no such thing as a free lunch. On average, building a house following the principles of building biology is about 10% more expensive. Though it is not a low-cost building method, the investment is worth it. Any additional costs will pay for themselves in the medium to long term, because this way of "healthy" building is committed to high standards and saving energy, and furthermore enhances the quality and joy of life.

I am very grateful to the author Nurgül Ece for her dedication and effort. I wish this book every success and hope readers will enjoy it. May it inspire others to create many more building biology projects.

Winfried Schneider
Architect and Managing Director
Institute of Building Biology + Sustainability IBN

7

A Book about Building Biology

With the knowledge we have today, we can create paradise on earth. Building biology is an important building block to reach this goal. This makes getting involved with building biology so rewarding.[1]

Architects have many different things to consider in the design of our built environment. They have to meet a broad range of demands: the client's financial budget, building codes and safety regulations, as well as the requirements of energy efficiency. They have a sociocultural responsibility, but at the same time are committed to creativity. Furthermore, people and the environment are at the very heart of their considerations. In this context, it becomes increasingly important to examine and reflect on what and how we plan, taking into consideration how the built environment affects us. After all, people in the modern Western world spend up to 90% of their time indoors. We live, work, play, and sleep in indoor environments. These should therefore be as pleasant, stimulating, and restorative as possible. As our third skin, the built environment provides shelter, thermal comfort, and security. The aspects of health and sustainability—clearly identified as trends by futurists—also play an important role. Global trends regarding food and clothing such as "organic," "regional," and "fair trade" are rapidly gaining momentum in the world of building, following the motto, "You've made your home, now live in it." It was Arthur Schopenhauer who said: "Health is not everything, but without health, everything is nothing."

As an architect, I would like to demonstrate that building biology offers everything needed to create a healthy and aesthetically appealing built environment. Prof. Dr. Anton Schneider, the pioneer of building biology, strongly believed that it is possible to live in harmony with nature in our built environment. To do so, he felt it necessary to raise the awareness of building culture to a higher, more natural level once again.[2] What this means and how to achieve it is illustrated in this book, which explains how architecture and building methods based on building biology can help save resources and support cradle-to-cradle product life cycles. The book also shows how buildings based on the principles of building biology implement holistic approaches to promote human health and well-being and at the same time features interesting examples of modern, contemporary architecture.

When we consider climate change, the migrations that result from it, but also the disputes over resources, the developments arising from these pressures of growth, progress, and consumption in globalized societies become clear. The effects of an economic model based on a foreign supply system[3] are felt worldwide. In response to this situation, we need appropriate strategies. The international community has addressed the subject with the United Nations (UN) climate conferences. Agenda 21[4] is a plan of action compiled by the UN for sustainable development. The European Union's Roadmap to a Resource Efficient Europe[5] outlines how to achieve significant changes in final energy consumption, the reduction of greenhouse gas emissions, the exploitation of raw materials, and the demand of water, by implementing better building methods and improving building use.

1 Prof. Dr. Anton Schneider, Building Biology Online Course IBN, Course Module 1, Chapter 4.
2 Ibid.
3 Nico Paech, "Befreiung vom Überfluss", 4th ed., Munich: Oekom Verlag, 2013, p. 63ff.
4 www.sustainabledevelopment.un.org/content/documents/Agenda21.pdf (accessed on 22 February 2017).
5 European Commission, The Roadmap to a Resource Efficient Europe, Chapter 5.2, Brussels, 2011.
6 www.sustainabledevelopment.un.org/content/documents/Agenda21.pdf (accessed on 22 February 2017); see Chapter 3.5, 5.42–43, 34.24.
7 www.nachhaltigkeit.info/artikel/mission_des_club_of_rome_540.htm (accessed on 23 February 2017).
8 Institute for Sustainable Urbanism at the Faculty of Architecture at the Technical University of Braunschweig; www.sustainableurbanism.de (accessed on 10 February 2017).
9 Institute for Design and Architectural Strategies at the Technical University of Braunschweig; www.idas.tu-bs./index.php (accessed on 10 February 2017).
10 Centre for Urban Ecology and Climate Adaptation at the Technical University of Munich; www.zsk.tum.de (accessed on 10 February 2017).
11 www.dienachwachsendestadt.org (accessed on 10 February 2017).
12 www.baubiologie.de/weiterbildung/fernlehrgang-baubiologie or www.buildingbiology.com/building-biology-course-ibn (accessed on 20 March 2017).

Another possibility, also established in Agenda 21,[6] is the idea of "think globally, act locally"[7]: To make a difference in the well-being of the world, we must show social responsibility and take individual action that supports local economic resilience. Therefore, building biology not only focuses on energy-efficient, sustainable, and healthy ways of building, but also considers socioecological and sociocultural aspects of life. To this end, building biology is incorporated into the strategies for sustainable transformation such as the transition town movement by Rob Hopkins, the cradle-to-cradle economy model by Michael Braungart and William McDonough, or the permaculture design by Bill Mollison and David Holmgren. My motto is: "The way we treat our environment defines how we treat each other." With my book, I would also like to encourage the discussion on how building biology should be incorporated into the scientific teachings at our universities. Interdisciplinary approaches are strongly encouraged in this field. All the strategies below show how research is already being conducted in similar fields: e.g. "Future Cities" by the Institute for Sustainable Urbanism (ISU),[8] "Hortitecture" for "Healthy, Livable Cities" by the Institute for Design and Architectural Strategies (IDAS)[9] of the TU Braunschweig, projects at the Centre for Urban Ecology and Climate Adaptation (ZSK)[10] of the TU Munich on the issue of what climate protection and climate adaptation could look like, and the study of the renewable city "Die Nachwachsende Stadt."[11]

Building Biology—Criteria and Architectural Design conveys the contents and principles of building biology. It is based on the teachings of the Institute of Building Biology and Sustainability IBN as offered through the state-approved Fernlehrgang Baubiologie IBN or Building Biology Online Course IBN.[12] This book explains criteria and approaches, spanning the past forty years of building biology to the architectural design of building biology projects today. It presents the basic knowledge and makes the subject of building biology accessible. With the IBN building in Rosenheim, a building project is introduced here that was completed with strict adherence to the principles of building biology; and then additional projects are presented and discussed from a building biology perspective to showcase design alternatives for different tasks.

Nurgül Ece
Architect, Building Biology Consultant IBN
Permaculture Designer

Introduction
to Building Biology

Building biology is defined as "the study of the holistic relationship between humans and their living and work environments." It is committed to human health, environmental sustainability, and preventive building measures and focuses on a humane and ecological way of building that strives to strike a balance between humans, the built environment, and nature.

Building biology focuses on a humane and ecological way of building that strives to strike a balance between humans, the built environment, and nature.

Figure 1
Factors that affect humans as well as the built and natural environment

These elements affect those elements:

These elements affect those elements	Physical health	Mental health	Toxic emissions / odors	Fibers / dust	Air humidity	Mold / bacteria	Electrosmog (ELF)	Electrosmog (RF)	Light and color – psychological	Noise / acoustics	Social environment / neighborhood	Building material selection / building method	Diffusion / humidity-regulating properties	Radioactivity / radon	Furniture / interior furnishings	Heating / thermal comfort	Ventilation	Residential / population density	Energy consumption / environmental performance
Physical health																			
Mental health																			
Toxic emissions / odors																			
Fibers / dust																			
Air humidity																			
Mold / bacteria																			
Electrosmog (ELF)																			
Electrosmog (RF)																			
Light and color – psychological																			
Noise / acoustics																			
Social environment / neighborhood																			
Building material selection / building method																			
Diffusion / humidity-regulating properties																			
Radioactivity / radon																			
Furniture / interior furnishings																			
Heating / thermal comfort																			
Ventilation																			
Residential/population density																			
Energy consumption / environmental performance																			

Criteria and Approaches

Building biology is defined as "the study of the holistic relationship between humans and their living and work environments."[1] The holistic approach is central to building biology and is applied in a comprehensive and integral manner to promote a healthy and sustainable way of building, housing, and living. Building biology is committed to human health, environmental sustainability, and preventive building measures.[2]

Sustainable and Holistic

As early as the 1970s, Anton Schneider coined the term "building biology." Initially, he was concerned with creating healthy living spaces and improving the quality of life. Later, he also integrated sustainability into the overall concept, including ecological and social aspects. Sustainability goes as far back as the eighteenth century, when it was first applied in forest management.[3] Foresters realized that the key properties of a natural system should be preserved for the long term. They harvested only as much timber as the forest would be able to regrow. Many years later, after the United Nations had hosted the first climate conferences, this approach was expanded, and in 1998 a concept of sustainability, which had already been in use by building biology, was drafted by the German federal government[4]: "To reconcile ecology and economy in such a way that the needs of the present generation are met without compromising the ability of future generations to meet their own needs."[5]

With this in mind, sustainable building[6] is based on ecological, economic, and social dimensions. The ecological dimension pursues the conservation of resources, the minimization of consumption of any type of medium and environmental hazards; the economic dimension considers the costs of acquisition, construction, operation, recycling, or disposal (life cycle assessment); and the sociocultural dimension covers design, aesthetics, accessibility, and human health. Due to its holistic approach, building biology considers not only additional health-relevant factors such as radiation biology (radio-, photo-, electro-, and geobiology) and architectural psychology, but also environmental protection. Figure 1 shows the factors that are considered in building biology.

In Harmony with Nature

In building biology, the origins of the term building biology are explained as follows: "All areas of biology (living organisms) and building (living environment) interact with each other under the direction of the logos (Greek. reason),"[7] or put another way: Building is done in harmony with nature (Figure 2).

Figure 2
Etymology

Building	Bios (Greek)	Logos (Greek)
Home, skin	Life	Word (word of god, judgment)
Home, Homeland	Life force	Creation (creative power)
Apartment	Related to nature	Incarnation, manifestation
Adaption	Living world	Ordering world-reason
Safety		World order, harmony, health, outer space, holism, culture
Hut, hat, shelter		Unity (mind-body-soul)

The 25 Principles of Building Biology
are a practical summary of building biology criteria.
They cover the areas of the building site, building
methods, indoor climate, interior design, and how to
deal with the environment, energy, and water.

Biological and Cultural

Building biology focuses on a humane and ecological way of building that strives to strike a balance between humans, the built environment, and nature. It also explores biological and cultural aspects: "... building biology-oriented architecture [combines] ... functionality with artistic aesthetics, a focus on health, and the integration of ecosocial aspects ..."[8] Humans are considered in their entirety here, which is why the subject areas are varied and range from urban coexistence in UrbanScapes[9] and ecosocial communities, where humans, the natural environment and culture are at the center of building and housing, to a healthy indoor climate, which promotes the occupants' well-being. They also include the promotion of skilled crafts and trades, the support for alternative housing concepts and work environments, as well as the application of the principles of architectural psychology with regard to space, color, and scale to nourish the soul. To protect the natural environment, it is also important to reduce energy consumption—be it primary or embodied energy or useful energy—and substances harmful to the environment by choosing untreated, renewable, and regional resources, renewable energies, as well as energy-efficient and resource-conscious building methods (Figure 3).

Interdisciplinary

Building biology is a complex field of many subject areas that are inherently interdisciplinary. These include architecture, building technology, building economics, and spatial planning, as well as disciplines in the fields of biology, ecology, medicine, chemistry, physics, geology, botany, physiology, sociology, and anthroposophy. Building biology thereby creates a new building culture. A number of building biology institutes are actively teaching building biology all around the world. The 25 Principles of Building Biology[10] are a practical summary of building biology criteria (see page 169). They cover the areas of the building site, building methods, indoor climate, interior design, and how to deal with the environment, energy, and water. The Standard of Building Biology Testing Methods (SBM)[11] provides an important complement. Many building biology statements can be demonstrated with the help of measurements and thus become scientifically verifiable.

Figure 3
Holistic building biology

Sustainable	Healthy	Well-designed
Energy-efficient building design	Healthy indoor climate	Nature as the standard
Renewable energies	No toxic emissions	Measurements, proportions, and shapes with respect for the human scale
No environmental problems	Reduced fungi/bacteria/dust/allergens	Architectural psychology
Regional	Reduced electrosmog	Natural light, lighting, colors
Ecosocial coexistence	Sound insulation to meet human needs	
Coexistence of living and working	Best possible air, light, and water quality	

Building Biology
and Natural Building Methods

With its biological and cultural approach, building biology also includes sensual and psychological considerations besides the engineering and physics aspects of building. Since our "third skin," our home, is meant to provide additional protection, thermal comfort, and security, it is important to build healthy homes that promote the occupants' well-being. Health is a fundamental part of our lives. We stay healthy through regular exercise, proper nutrition, and a good work–life balance; we also pay attention to the origins of our food and clothing as well as their raw materials and manufacturing processes. Building biology is a tool with which we can evaluate our built environment according to similar ethical standards regarding health, sustainability, social responsibility, and aesthetics. In this way, building biology can help us lead satisfying, pleasant, and healthy lives with respect for the natural environment.

Natural building methods based on the principles of building biology respect the human scale. They create a sense of orientation, variety, and harmony, and make personalized individuality possible, while fostering community living, mixed-use developments, and self-sufficient lifestyles close to nature. This holistic approach allows materials to be treated and processed according to their inherent qualities and promotes artistic design in building. A building not only has to protect its occupants against wind and weather, but also provide space for creativity and purpose. Such a building creates a healthy indoor climate, blends well with its surroundings, and fulfills ecological requirements to ensure that it can meet the owner's needs and those of society.

Figure 4
Building materials

Wood	Masonry	
Log construction	Sand-lime bricks	
Round logs	Autoclaved aerated concrete blocks	
Wood beams	Clay bricks	
Mass timber construction	Perforated bricks	
Solid wood wall – no adhesives	Solid bricks	
Cross-laminated timber (CLT)		
Dowel-laminated timber (DLT)	Clay	Straw
Hollow timber systems	Rammed earth	Straw bales
	Adobe	Masonry blocks
Heavy timber construction	Clay-filled hose	Infill in heavy timber construction
Mass timber	Clay board	Straw insulation
KVH solid structural timber	Clay plaster	Bales
Duo and trio beams	Light clay	As an additive
Glued-laminated timber (glulam)	Infill	
Thermally modified wood	Insulation	
Wood products	In rammed earth walls	

Building Materials[12]

When implementing natural building methods, all legal requirements and regulations of building codes and standards must be followed. All state-specific building codes in Germany contain the following clause: "Building structures ... are to be located, built, altered, and maintained in such a way that public safety and order, in particular, life, health, and natural resources are not compromised."[13]

Building activities that follow the principles of building biology encourage the use of healthy and sustainable building materials and elements. The design principles employed and the building materials used are explained below (see Figure 4).

Wood Construction

Wood construction is often used in building biology projects. As a renewable building material, wood is used as a structural element in heavy timber construction and in solid wood construction. In terms of building biology and building science, the most important principles of quality of wood construction are: (a) the use of lumber that is as dry as possible (< 18% WMC), including the respective performance requirements according to DIN EN 15497, (b) the elimination of chemical wood preservatives in compliance with DIN 68800, (c) the reduction of electromagnetic pollution as much as possible, and (d) the elimination of adhesive- or metal-based connections wherever possible.

In addition to providing proper thermal, sound, and fire protection, sourcing regionally harvested wood from sustainable forests is a must for achieving good environmental performance. Where the origins of the wood are unknown, certification labels such as FSC, PEFC, or "Holz von hier" are useful. In the case of wood products, however, their sustainability and recyclability strongly depend on the binders and additives used. When wood is not sealed and its pores remain open to diffusion, its special properties—vapor-permeable, hygroscopic, and heat-storing—contribute to a healthy indoor climate.

Masonry Construction

Masonry construction—as a load-bearing alternative in combination with heavy timber construction or as a ceiling system—is also used in building biology projects. The manufacturing process of making bricks is usually more energy intensive. Many bricks, however, have great structural and technical properties. Clays and earths, the basic raw materials of bricks, support a great indoor climate. Sand-lime bricks, which have good environmental performance and favorable sound insulation, can also be used. Autoclaved aerated concrete blocks have good environmental performance too, and—in contrast to sand-lime bricks—provide good thermal insulation. In masonry construction that follows the principles of building biology, the following materials should be avoided: polystyrene- or mineral fiber-based fillings, isocyanate-based PU adhesives, plasters with synthetic resins, algicides, or fungicides.

Earth Construction

In building biology, unburned clay is the preferred building material in masonry construction. Clay can be used as adobe bricks (load-bearing and as infill), also as rammed earth, clay plaster, or light clay (clay mixed with organic or mineral-based additives to provide better thermal insulation). As a natural material, clay has specific properties as it is not water-resistant, but fire-resistant. During the drying process, shrinkage occurs, but clay in its dry state also preserves, for example, wood by keeping it dry. As light clay, it shows good thermal insulation. Clay promotes an excellent indoor climate by binding with toxins in the air and removing them as well as by being vapor-permeable and hygroscopic. For quality assurance purposes, the composition of the clay and the structural design details must be carefully considered.

Building materials made from clay are now regulated in DIN standards (DIN 18945–18947). If clay products are made on the construction site, the German clay building regulations still apply. As with all masonry building materials, the radioactivity of clay can be elevated. A building biology assessment of the property, house, or material in question can determine the level of radioactivity. Well-known building material manufacturers generally ensure that their products do not show elevated levels of radioactivity. The German Association for Building with Earth recommends that testing for radioactivity should be included in the DIN standards.[14]

Straw Bale Construction

Straw bales are another special building material that has now received certification through building authorities. Straw bale construction comes in two main forms: solid walls, the most common form, or as infill for heavy timber construction. The fire resistance of straw bales is achieved by covering the walls with plaster. This also protects the straw against moisture, insects, and rodents. The thermal insulation capacity of straw is high. Straw, of course, is also vapor-permeable.

Reinforced Concrete Construction

From a building biology perspective, it is noteworthy that the vapor permeability, sorption capacity, and hygroscopicity of common steel or steel-reinforced concrete construction are rather low. This type of construction takes a relatively long time to dry, poses electromagnetic risks, and is highly thermally conductive. The manufacturing of steel and concrete is very energy-intensive and, in the case of fire, the expansion properties of steel can cause it to buckle. It is possible to create structures from the above-mentioned materials as an alternative to steel and reinforced concrete construction, while at the same time meeting building regulations. Buildings such as the LCT ONE Tower in Dornbirn (Austria), the Brock Commons student residence in Vancouver (Canada), the H8 in Bad Aibling (Germany), or the HoHo Wien in Vienna (Austria) illustrate that wood construction, partly as hybrid systems, has now become competitive in terms of building economics. The exhibition A New Way of Building with Wood—Paths into the Future concluded: A little over a third of the German timber harvest would be sufficient to build —in wood— all the new buildings built in Germany in a single year.[15]

Natural building methods based on building biology principles respect the human scale. They create a sense of orientation, variety, and harmony and make personalized individuality possible, while fostering community living, mixed-use developments, and self-sufficient lifestyles close to nature.

Thermal Insulation

Due to current requirements regarding energy efficiency and airtightness such as the German Energy Saving Ordinance (EnEV), thermal insulation is important. External thermal insulation composite systems that receive the building biology seal of approval are open to diffusion and hygroscopic, form no toxic gases in the event of fire, can be easily disposed of, and are primarily made of renewable or mineral resources (see Figure 5). Most renewable insulation materials have good hygroscopic properties (see Figure 6). Owing to the capillary action in these materials, moisture can be wicked away and the risk of condensation between solid building materials and the insulation can be minimized.

Thermal protection against the heat in summer is also important. To achieve this, the insulation materials in the building envelope not only need to feature a good thermal insulation capacity (low k-value, high R-value) but a matching high thermal storage capacity (s) and thus a low thermal diffusivity (a). As an alternative, a building envelope that provides great thermal insulation can be combined with materials on the inside that offer great thermal storage.

Costs

Because building projects whose design is based on the principles of building biology often use higher-quality materials and installation methods, building costs are generally higher (by about 10%). As a result of the use of more durable materials, the implementation of more energy-efficient building methods, and consideration for the occupants' health, any additional costs will pay for themselves within just a few years. The following strategies can reduce additional costs caused by the requirements of building biology and energy efficiency:

Compact, simple design with optimized floor plans, structural design, and construction type

Simple installation and technologies

Choosing good, cost-conscious building designers and skilled tradespeople

Contributing personal labor (in the case of residential homeowners)

Collaborative projects such as two-family houses, tenant groups, and eco-communities

Furthermore, building activities that follow the principles of building biology also contribute to society as a whole and the economy, because considerable cost savings can be realized in environmental protection, health care, and old-age security, as health symptoms and treatments can be reduced.

Figure 5
Thermal insulation materials

Thermal insulation							
Organic				Mineral			
Wood		Plant	Animal				
Blown-in	Boards			Board	Loose fill	Additive	
Wood wool	Wood wool board	Cotton	Sheep wool	Foam glass	Perlite	Perlite	
Wood fiber	Wood fiber insulation board	Coconut fiber		Calcium silicate	Expanded glass	Expanded glass	
Cellulose	Soft fiberboard	Reed		Aerated concrete		Expanded clay	
		Flax					
		Hemp					

Assessment scores		Thermal behavior	Moisture behavior	Diffusion s_d	Toxicity	Manufacture	Disposal	Fire behavior	Overall assessment*
0	Not relevant or neutral								
–	Negative								
––	Very negative/alarming								
+	Positive								
++	Very advantageous								
Thermal insulation material									
1	Polyurethane PUR, l = 0.030	+	––	––	––	––	––	––	–11
2	Polystyrene EPS+XPS, l = 0.035	+	––	––	––	––	––	––	–10
3	Fiberglass/mineral wool, l = 0.035	+	––	++	––	––	––	+	–4
4	Polyester, l = 0.040	+	––	++	0	–	–	–	–2
5	Sheep wool (batt), l = 0.040	+	+	++	–	–	+	–	2
6	Cotton (batt), l = 0.040	+	0	++	0	–	+	–	2
7	Flax, hemp (batt), l = 0.040	+	+	++	0	0	+	–	4
8	Cellulose fiber, l = 0.045	+	+	++	–	0	+	0	4
9	Low-density fiberboards, l = 0.045	++	++	++	0	–	++	0	8
10	Baked cork, l = 0.045	+	0	++	0	–	++	–	3
11	Coconut fiber, l = 0.045	+	++	++	0	–	+	–	5
12	Reed, l = 0.055	+	+	++	0	0	++	–	5
13	Foam glass, l = 0.050	+	0	0	0	–	+	++	3
14	Calcium silicate board, l = 0.050	+	++	++	0	–	+	++	7
15	Perlite, l = 0.050	+	–	++	–	–	0	++	2
16	Straw bales, l = 0.045	+	+	++	0	0	++	–	5
17	Blown-in wood fiber insulation, l = 0.040	++	++	++	0	0	++	–	6
18	Expanded mica, l = 0.070	0	–	++	0	–	+	++	4
19	Wood wool board, l ≥ 0.075	0	++	++	0	–	+		5
20	Expanded clay, l ≥ 0.080	–	+	++	0	–	+	++	4

Figure 6
Building biology assessment of thermal insulation materials

* Sum total of positive and negative scores

Notes

A Assessment of thermal insulation and storage capacity
B Assessment of hygroscopic properties and drying periods
C Assessment of water vapor permeability – diffusion properties sd-value/ diffusion equivalent air layer thickness in m
D Assessment of air pollutants as well as fibers
E Assessment of the manufacturing conditions (ecological, toxicological, and social) including working conditions, energy requirements, transportation, processing, and availability. Prefer renewable (and to a certain extent mineral-based materials available in large amounts) resources.
F Assessment of waste management issues and the possibility of reuse and/or reprocessing (also in terms of raw material extraction, production, transportation, and processing)
G Assessment of flammability, toxicity issues in the case of fire, and smoke behavior

The checklist makes the most sense in the context of the Building Biology Online Course IBN. Depending on the various manufacturers, all values may vary. Not all listed insulation materials are currently officially approved as such.

1 Polyols, polyisocyanates, flame retardant = tris(2-chlorisopropyl)phosphate or HBCD (hexabromcyclododecane), expanding agent = pentane, CO_2
2 Polystyrene, flame retardant = HBCD (hexabromcyclododecane), expanding agent = pentane, CO_2
3 Phenol formaldehyde resin 0% to 8%
5 Impregnation at times with urea derivatives and at times with reinforcing polyester fibers; untreated = risk of moth infestation
6 Treated with ca. 2% borates
7 Treated with borates or soda, at times with reinforcing fibers made of polyester or plant starch
8 Made from recycled paper, ca. 15% borates
9 Wet-processed low-density fiberboards: at times 0.5% aluminum sulfate, 0.5% alum, ca. 0.8% PVAC glue in glue-laminated boards, in water-repellent boards, ca. 10% to 15% bitumen, latex or paraffin
11 Flame retardant ammonium sulfate, borates, sodium silicate; latex coating for moisture-prone areas
12 Generally bound with wire
13 Foamed silicates, foaming agent CO_2
14 Calcium silicate + cellulose, foamed with water vapor
15 Expanded perlite, 0.02% silicone, partially natural resins, bitumen
16 Fire and insect protection required
17 At times, clay the only additive; currently treated, among others, with ammonium sulfate and borates
18 Aluminum iron silicate, expanded, e.g, bitumen
19 Magnesite- or cement-bonded

Energy-Efficient Building Design

From a holistic perspective, energy-efficient building[16] is the synthesis of sustainability criteria related to human health and the environment. These criteria include a well-balanced level of thermal storage and insulation, well-matched surface and indoor air temperatures, the use of radiant heat for heating, and of course, the use of renewable energy sources. Aside from the building code requirements to reduce heat loss, there are many strategies that contribute to energy savings: a building design that is appropriate for a given climate and site, the selection of suitable building systems, heat gains from solar heat, and informed user behavior regarding heating and ventilation.

Renewable Energies

Most renewable energy sources used in buildings are based on solar power. Electricity can be generated by solar cells (photovoltaic energy), and heat for hydronic heating systems and domestic hot water can be collected using solar collectors (solar thermal energy). The ambient heat from the air, ground, or water, which is utilized by heat pump systems to provide heat to buildings, is also indirectly supplied by solar energy. Another option to use ambient heat is the extraction of geothermal energy from deep earth strata.

The passive use of solar heat in buildings is facilitated by aligning the orientation of the building with the corresponding floor plan zoning, transparent glazing, and thermal mass.

Energy-Efficient Design

A building design that reduces, for example, the number of heated room surfaces, orientates the building to the south, and defines warm core zones by locating buffer rooms to the north (in temperate climate zones), saves energy. In the detailed design stage, structural measures should include the elimination of thermal bridges, improving the airtightness of the building envelope, and the optimization of the thermal insulation.

The consumption of conventional energy sources can be reduced by energy-aware behavior, the addition of insulation, the optimized use of passive and active solar energy, as well as the implementation of an efficient heating and ventilation concept. In this process, it is always important to work with building materials that were produced in an energy-efficient manner (good environmental performance) and are recommended in building biology guidelines. Because every building project is unique, it is also recommended that experts, e.g. Building Biology Energy Advisors IBN, are consulted to assess the project both at an individual level and in a holistic context.

Figure 7
Factors that affect the indoor climate

Air	Temperature	Humidity	Electroclimate
Composition	Radiant heat	Air humidity	ELF electric fields
Dust level	Thermal conduction	Material moisture	ELF magnetic fields
Fungi, bacteria, allergens	Thermal insulation	Condensation	Radio-frequency radiation
Odors	Convection	Isolation	Static electric fields
Movement	Surface temperature	Hygroscopic properties	Static magnetic fields
Diffusion	Exterior / interior temperatures	Vapor diffusion	Earth's magnetic field
Ventilation	Heating / air conditioning		Air ionization (static electricity)
Air pressure	Sun		
	Heat currents		

Healthy Indoor Climate

One of the most important aspects of building biology focuses on the healthy indoor climate.[17] It defines the value of a building in relation to the users' health and comfort. And regarding a positive atmosphere at work, a healthy indoor climate also has a beneficial impact on work performance. A wide range of factors have an impact on indoor climate: the building materials, the type of construction, installations and furnishings, as well as the type of settlement and exterior climate conditions. Indoor climate is also affected by temperature, humidity, air, and electroclimate (Figure 7).

Temperature

The temperatures of the air and interior surfaces of a given space are very important because sufficiently high interior surface temperatures are crucial to thermal comfort. In Figure 8, the temperature range of the thermal comfort zone is shown in relation to the temperatures of the indoor air and wall surfaces.

According to the thermal comfort chart, the floor, wall, and ceiling surfaces should ideally be max. 2 °C lower or max. 5 °C higher than the air in the room. To achieve surface temperatures that are as warm as possible, the thermal properties of the building materials—especially their thermal conductivity and storage characteristics—should be considered, because those are the factors that determine the speed at which surfaces heat up. Besides the building materials themselves, surface heating systems, but also surface cooling systems, can be instrumental in creating optimal surface temperatures. Surfaces that are too cold are associated with the additional risk of condensation and thus moisture and mold problems. Furthermore, each 1 °C increase in indoor air temperature due to cold surfaces translates into an increase of about 5% to 6% in heating costs.

Air Humidity and Dust

Air humidity is another important indicator of a healthy indoor climate. A relative air humidity level of 40% to 60% is considered ideal by medical and building biology standards. Apart from the air and surface temperatures, air humidity is also determined by the type of heating system, the ventilation rate, the choice of building materials, the number of occupants and their activities in the room, and of course, the outdoor climate. Dry air contains and leads to more airborne dust. Dust often also contains toxic substances and microorganisms that are inhaled with the indoor air. Furthermore, dry air increases the buildup of static electricity on synthetic surfaces, which in turn changes the naturally occurring slightly negative ionization of the air.

Negatively charged air is relevant to human health because, among other things, it stabilizes breathing, improves blood composition, and stimulates the metabolism. Conversely, positively charged air impairs the respiratory function in such a way that, together with dust, pathogens can more easily lodge themselves in the respiratory system. The best way to influence air humidity is by providing proper ventilation and using moisture-absorbing or hygroscopic materials that can buffer the fluctuating humidity levels in the air. In addition, a building method that is also open to diffusion provides another natural strategy to reduce potential mold growth.

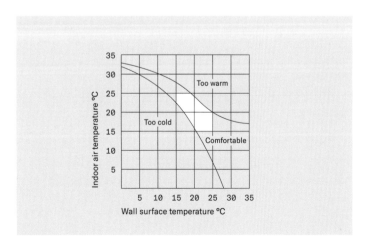

Figure 8
Temperature and thermal comfort:
correlation between mean
indoor air temperature and wall surface
temperature

To maintain a comfortable and healthy indoor climate in the long term, no pollutant-emitting or synthetic materials should be chosen for interior surfaces and furnishings.

Ventilation and Heating

Ventilation and heating also have a major impact on indoor climate. Sufficient air exchange removes moisture and pollutants, increases the oxygen level, especially the negatively charged oxygen ions, and reduces odors and the concentration of microorganisms in the air. The easiest way to maintain comfortable surface temperatures is the use of a surface heating system that provides a high level of radiant heat. Such a system also leads to less air and dust circulation, while at the same time avoiding odor problems and noise pollution.

Materials

To maintain a comfortable and healthy indoor climate in the long term, no pollutant-emitting or synthetic materials should be chosen for interior surfaces and furnishings. Preference should be given to untreated, vapor-permeable, and hygroscopic materials that have a high sorption capacity and do not affect the balance of the natural electroclimate. The thermal conductivity and storage capacity of the materials should also be considered. Natural products and materials are well suited here. The range of possible materials includes:

Wood in any form for surfaces and furniture
PVC-free linoleum for flooring
Natural stones and tiles with low radioactivity
Plasters and finishes based on clay, silicate, and lime
Waxes, stains, and oil finishes with natural resins for surface treatments
Stainless steel, ceramics, glass, or tadelakt for wet rooms, bathrooms, and kitchens
Untreated wood, willow, rattan, and bamboo for furniture frames
Straw, coconut fiber, wool, kapok, flax, horsehair, jute, hemp, linen, and natural latex for upholstery and mattresses
Sisal, coir, hemp, and wool for textile floor coverings
Untreated cotton, linen, hemp, and vegetable-tanned leather for covers

As a rule, building materials should always be checked for their ingredients. Building material databases such as WECOBIS, the Swiss Bauprodukte Deklaration (building material declaration) by SIA, or the Austrian baubook, provide information about categories of building materials. Libraries of building components such as the LEGEP building component library, the baubook calculator for building components, the Swiss building component library, and the British Green Guide to Specification are also good research resources. In German-speaking countries, the composition of building products can be verified by, for example, the following certifications and seals: DINB, Natureplus, GIBBeco, IBR, or eco-INSTITUT. At the end of this chapter (Figure 25), the "Checklist for Building Materials" offers a condensed version of building biology assessments. If in doubt or if the building material has already been installed, a building biology professional should and could also be consulted.

Building Biology and Building Systems

Heating System[18]

From a building biology perspective, systems with radiant heat are ideal for both health and economic reasons because this type of heat is equivalent to the infrared heat from the sun that warms our planet Earth. Figure 9 illustrates that radiant heat is perceived as more comfortable, and Figure 10 reveals that the temperature gradients are much lower, which is especially relevant for buildings with poor thermal insulation.

The source of the radiant heat can be a traditional masonry heater or tiled stove, or it can be a conventional central heating system with heat generator, heat storage and distribution, and heat use. Heat can be generated with a biomass boiler (e.g. pellets, split logs, or chips), a condensing gas boiler, masonry heater, heat pump or combined heat and power system. In those systems, the heat stored in the buffer storage tank is normally distributed through a hydronic piping system to the individual heating units (ideally with a high percentage of radiant heat ≥ 60%) or surface heating panels embedded in walls, floors, or ceilings.

Baseboard heating or modern hypocaust systems can also be used as surface heating systems. This form of heat supply, which may be more accurately referred to as temperature control, is often sufficient to "heat" new, typically airtight houses. Due to their low supply temperatures, these low-temperature heating systems offer the additional advantage of using available emission-free and sustainable energy sources such as solar energy and ambient or geothermal energy.

In addition to heating and ventilation, the other building systems regarding the use of water, electricity, energy, daylight, and lighting are extremely important to building biology considerations.

Figure 10
Heating system based on convection (top)
or on radiant heat (bottom)

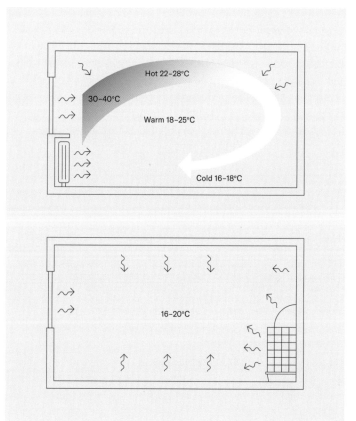

Figure 9
Thermal comfort through convection and radiation

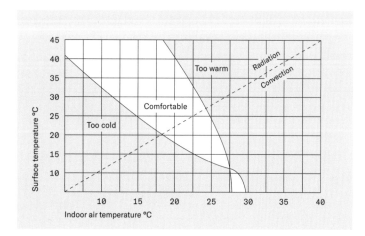

In addition to heating and ventilation, the other building systems regarding the use of water, electricity, energy, daylight, and lighting are extremely important to building biology considerations.

Ventilation System[19]

The airtight way of building often requires a ventilation concept to ensure that the structure is protected against moisture, pollutants are removed, and sufficient fresh air is supplied, without losing too much heat in the process. If one reviews energy consumption (Figure 11), it becomes obvious that individual heating and ventilation habits have a greater impact on consumption than thermal insulation or the use of solar energy.

Air exchange can be facilitated not only by natural ventilation and decentralized trickle vents, but also through controlled mechanical ventilation with different components; Figure 12 shows the various options. If the decision is made to use a mechanical ventilation system, professional design and installation as well as regular maintenance are important to avoid hygiene- and noise-related problems. The required electricity should come from renewable energy sources (e.g. photovoltaic energy or green power), and the system should have a control center that allows for individual settings and flexibility of use (e.g. optional setting for natural ventilation). In the case of natural ventilation, it is the user who determines the efficiency of the system through his or her ventilation behavior, with cross ventilation being the most efficient strategy.

Plumbing System[20]

Water is crucial in building biology, not least because of its ecosocial aspect. Drinking water is a "survival food," just like air and other basic foods. The unequal global distribution of drinking water is increasingly becoming a problem.[21] From a building biology perspective, this makes both the provision of hygienically safe water and strategies for the reduction of fresh water consumption important.

The German Drinking Water Regulation (TrinkwV) regulates the safeguarding of human health and ensures that water for human consumption is potable and pure. Since water quality is the responsibility of the homeowner after entering the building, certain criteria should be considered. For hygiene reasons, the water distribution system as well as the supply lines (hot and cold water) to the kitchen and the hot water tank should be made of stainless steel or galvanized copper. To avoid microbial contamination (e.g. Legionella bacteria or bacterial film), hot water at 70 °C should be run through the piping after stagnation periods. The following strategies can help save energy: avoid lime scale, favour a decentralized system for the hot water supply, insulate the piping and storage tanks, choose short pipe runs, and in central systems, optimize the running time of the circulation pumps. Conservation of water without sacrificing comfort is possible through the more conscious use of water as a resource, but also through the use of water-efficient fixtures and appliances, gray water and rainwater, and ultimately through the installation of a urine-diverting dry toilet (UDDT). In new construction, separate pipes should be installed for wastewater and sewage water (containing fecal matter) to allow for the direct and/or later use of gray water.

Figure 11
Energy consumption

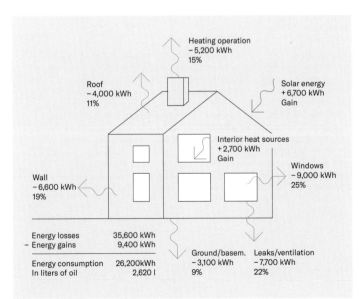

Heating operation
−5,200 kWh
15%

Roof
−4,000 kWh
11%

Solar energy
+6,700 kWh
Gain

Interior heat sources
+2,700 kWh
Gain

Windows
−9,000 kWh
25%

Wall
−6,600 kWh
19%

Energy losses	35,600 kWh
Energy gains	9,400 kWh
Energy consumption	26,200kWh
In liters of oil	2,620 l

Ground/basem.
−3,100 kWh
9%

Leaks/ventilation
−7,700 kWh
22%

Figure 12
Residential ventilation systems

Calculated air infiltration		
Natural ventilation		
Cross ventilation (moisture protection)	Cross ventilation	Stack ventilation
Fan-integrated ventilation		
Exhaust systems	Supply systems	Exhaust/ supply systems

Electric System[22]

In building biology, indoor electromagnetic quality is the key health factor with regard to electrical installations. It includes static electric and magnetic fields, power-frequency electric and magnetic fields, as well as radio-frequency radiation, radioactivity, radon, and geological disturbances. During the course of evolution, the human body has adapted to the naturally occurring background radiation on Earth. Developments in today's high-tech age, however, have caused major changes in the influence of natural electromagnetic fields. The way of life in urban centers, the spread of wireless radiation (radio masts and towers), as well as the careless use of electricity, can have damaging effects on our bodies. This can be traced back not only to a lack of exposure to naturally occurring electromagnetic fields such as the Earth's magnetic field, atmospheric electricity, and microwave radiation from space, but also to radiation stress, arising from exposure to power-frequency electric and magnetic fields, wireless radiation, and unnatural static fields; but also to radiation stress arising from exposure to power-frequency electric and magnetic fields, radio-frequency radiation, and unnatural static fields; Figure 13 provides an overview of the relevant frequencies of the electromagnetic spectrum.

Medical science has discovered that life processes of the human body are controlled by a variety of weak electromagnetic fields. According to the laws of physics, higher energy oscillations trigger lower energy oscillations. As a result, the electrically charged particles inside the human body will align to the external fields such as radio-frequency radiation exposure, causing the former to oscillate and go into resonance. The stress response will be triggered and, in the case of cumulative exposure, a wide range of symptoms may develop. This means that artificially generated electromagnetic fields or electrosmog always affect life processes. The relevant fields are listed below.

Static electric fields, also referred to as static electricity, occur where the free flow of electric charges is impeded, that is, at insulators, which are mostly synthetic materials, or at unshielded electric devices. As the static electric charges build up and the associated static electric fields increase, discharge will occur under certain conditions. As a result, the ionization of the breathing air changes and the indoor air quality declines.

Static magnetic fields occur at ferromagnetic metals or arise from direct currents. They distort and are superimposed on the Earth's naturally occurring magnetic field.

Extremely low frequency (ELF) electric fields arise from alternating current voltage, which is present in live wiring even if no appliance is switched on. In building wiring systems, poor workmanship can lead to potential differences, stray currents, and net currents, which in turn induce currents in the exposed occupants.

ELF magnetic fields arise from the flow of an alternating current. Artificial ELF electric and magnetic fields induce currents in the body and cause disturbances (see Figure 14). Studies show that these power-frequency fields are possibly carcinogenic to humans.[23]

Electromagnetic waves in the radio-frequency (RF) range from 3 kHz to 300 GHz are used for the wireless transmission of information and other radio applications. Radio-frequency radiation travels at the speed of light, but not only does it transmit the intended information, it also exposes human tissue to the radiation that goes into resonance. Today, humans in modern societies are exposed to significantly higher levels of RF radiation than only a hundred years ago. Studies show that the pulsed ELF signals of RF radiation have the most critical effects on the human body. Affected body systems include the regulatory systems of the nervous and endocrine systems, the immune system, and cell communication: e.g. measurable changes in brain wave activity, the clumping of red blood cells (so-called rouleaux formation), and the opening of the blood-brain barrier. Studies show that these radio-frequency fields are also possibly carcinogenic to humans.[24]

Figure 13
Frequencies of the
electromagnetic spectrum

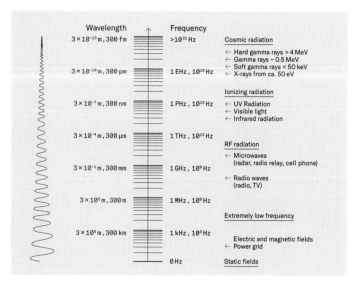

Wavelength		Frequency	
3×10^{-13} m, 300 fm		>10^{21} Hz	Cosmic radiation
			← Hard gamma rays > 4 MeV
			← Gamma rays ~ 0.5 MeV
			← Soft gamma rays < 50 keV
3×10^{-10} m, 300 pm		1 EHz, 10^{18} Hz	← X-rays from ca. 50 eV
			Ionizing radiation
3×10^{-7} m, 300 nm		1 PHz, 10^{15} Hz	← UV Radiation
			← Visible light
			← Infrared radiation
3×10^{-4} m, 300 µm		1 THz, 10^{12} Hz	RF radiation
			← Microwaves (radar, radio relay, cell phone)
3×10^{-1} m, 300 mm		1 GHz, 10^{9} Hz	← Radio waves (radio, TV)
3×10^{2} m, 300 m		1 MHz, 10^{6} Hz	Extremely low frequency
3×10^{5} m, 300 km		1 kHz, 10^{3} Hz	Electric and magnetic fields ← Power grid
		0 Hz	Static fields

Medical science has discovered that life processes of the human body are controlled by a variety of weak electromagnetic fields.

In building biology, it is very important to reduce or eliminate exposure to electromagnetic fields during periods of rest and recovery, especially during sleep, so that the human body is given a chance to regenerate at night. Nature always serves as a role model.

By following building biology recommendations for the installation of electrical wiring systems, elevated exposure levels can be avoided. The building wiring layout, for example, preferably follows a star-like pattern. Thus magnetic field exposure can already be reduced or eliminated by running dedicated circuits to specific rooms. Proper installation of the main equipotential bonding bar and the grounding system is essential; all electrically conductive parts and circuits must be connected here. It is possible to create zero-exposure areas for periods of rest and sleep by careful design of the wiring layout and placement of outlets/switches and the use of shielded wiring, or by integrating demand/cutoff switches that enable circuits to be turned off for certain periods of time.

There are also simple actions users can take to lower their exposure by following safer use guidelines and by doing without constantly transmitting wireless antennas such as cell phones, DECT cordless phones, Bluetooth, or Wi-Fi, especially during periods of rest and sleep. RF radiation exposure levels can be lowered by selecting appropriate materials and installing shielding. It is important to take preventive measures to minimize health risks.

Figure 14
ELF magnetic fields

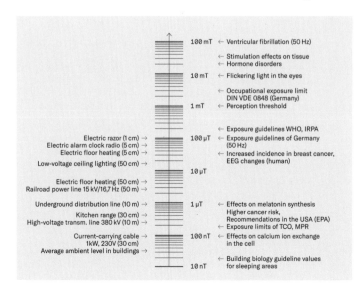

Light is an essential part of life. Sunlight determines human physical and mental well-being. Light is not just energy, it also triggers emotions and creates the perception of three dimensions and space by casting shade.

Daylight

From a building biology perspective, the quality of a building is defined by a lighting design that pursues daylight autonomy. This autonomy depends on the season, the building orientation, as well as the window and room geometry. To provide good daylighting, the visible light transmittance (VLT) of the glazing must be high and the solar heat gain coefficient (SHGC) or g-value must be low. In building biology projects, the daylight factor should be significantly higher than the average of 0.90% as defined in the German standard of Daylight in Interiors (DIN 5034). The room layout should follow the natural course of daylight, if possible. For example, it is recommended that bedrooms face east and living spaces face south and west so that the occupants' daily routine is in sync with the daily cycle of daylight. Glare and solar controls—also as protection against the heat in summer—should be adjusted according to the prevailing conditions.

Artificial Light

Artificial light ideally replicates natural daylight conditions as much as possible. The light color and light intensity of artificial lighting should approximate sunlight and be flicker-free. Flicker is described as periodic fluctuations in the brightness of emitted light, which are mostly invisible to the human eye, but may cause stress in humans. Furthermore, a high color rendering index (CRI) of the light source is useful for good illumination of the interior and the furnishings, preferably above 90.

Different types of lamps offer different types of light qualities:

Halogen lamps have great CRI values and are flicker-free.

Discharge lamps (fluorescent or compact fluorescent lamps) are considered problematic in building biology because they often have poor light quality and contain mercury. Due to ballasts, they emit electromagnetic fields and often flicker.

LED lamps are available in different qualities. Good-quality LED lamps are long-lasting, energy-efficient, and mostly flicker-free, while the color rendering index can range from acceptable to good (state-of-the-art technology: CRI > 90). Electronic drivers, especially those with a dimming function, can cause pulsing and thus flickering.

Life expectancy and energy consumption are important aspects of sustainability for artificial lighting as well. The selection criteria for lamps and light sources should include considerations for health, light quality, and life expectancy. The proportion of energy used for light in German private households was 2% for 2015 according to preliminary statistical calculations.[25] In commercial buildings, different requirements often have to be considered. Building biology recommendations include the following considerations: Constant exposure to too little light can lead to depression, pessimism, and melancholy; conversely, chronic exposure to too much light can lead to irritability, insomnia, neuroses, and phobias. Easy transitions between brightness and darkness strengthen and promote vitality, optimism, and compassion.

Pollutants and Allergens²⁶

Air pollutants damage ecosystems and cause human disease because foreign substances in the air contaminate crops and the soil and also enter the body. In our modern society, everybody is exposed to a wide range of products containing hazardous substances, which are also found in indoor environments. It is the goal of building biology to avoid or minimize substances harmful to human health.

Occurrence

Indoor exposure is often caused by the building itself as well as the furnishings, ventilation, air conditioning, and the use of it. Elevated exposure levels and anomalies due to local background levels are somewhat rare. Radon, a radioactive soil gas, for example, can be elevated. If the local radon level of the building site is elevated and there are leaks in the sections of the building in contact with the soil, radon can enter the building and accumulate. Radon exposure levels can be reduced by sealing entry routes and adjusting the ventilation accordingly.

Indoor air pollutants are divided and classified into the following categories according to Figure 15. These pollutants are found in many different products in indoor environments (see Figures 16–18). These often toxic substances enter the body through breathing (inhalation via the lungs), dermal contact (absorption via skin or mucous membranes), and/or food and water intake (oral ingestion including the digestive system).

* According to WHO   ** in the ordinary course of breathing air

Figure 15
Classification of air pollutants

Group of pollutants		Occurrence	Boiling point*	Type	Pollutants
VVOC	Very volatile organic compounds	Air	0°-100°	Solvents	Aromatic compounds, e.g. benzene, alcohol, aldehydes, ketones, esters
VOC	Volatile organic compounds	Air	50°-260°	Solvents	Chlorinated, halogenated compounds, e.g. tetrachloroethylene/perchloroethylene, aliphatic compounds, cyclical, olefinic hydrocarbon compounds Glycol compounds, siloxanes, and terpenes
				Formaldehyde Isocyanates	
SVOC	Semivolatile organic compounds	Air, dust**	240°-400°	Pesticides	Wood preservatives, e.g. lindane Insecticides, e.g. permethrin
				Flame retardants Plasticizers PAH, PCB	
MVOC	Microbial volatile organic compounds	Dust, air, surface		Molds Yeasts Bacteria	
POM	Particulate organic matter	Dust, surface	ab 380°	Fibers Fine part. matter Particulates Allergens	Asbestos, manmade mineral fibers (MMMF) Nanoparticles Mites, pollen, animal hair, pharmaceuticals
Radon		Air, material		Radioactive gas	
Heavy metals		Material		Metals	Arsenic, lead cadmium, chromium, cobalt, copper, nickel, mercury, thallium zinc, tin amalgam
				Metal salts Metal oxides Organometal. comp.	chromium (VI) tributyltin compounds
Harmful gases		Air		Irritant gases Asphyxiant gases	Sulfur dioxide, ozone, carbon monoxide, carbon dioxide

Figures 16/17
Volatile and semivolatile organic compounds in products
(individual substances in italics)

Product, source	Volatile organic compounds possibly found in
Dispersion paints	Glycols, alcohols
Scented oils	Terpenes (pinenes, carenes, limonenes), alcohols
Woodworking materials	Phenols, terpenes, aldehydes, formaldehyde
Adhesives	Aromatics, esters, ketones, isocyanates, aliphatic compounds
Cork	*Phenols, aldehydes, formaldehyde, furfural*
Parquet oils	Aliphates (naphtha, mostly unscented)
Parquet adhesives (old)	*Naphthalene, phenols, cresols*
Synthetic resin varnishes	Aromatics (toluene, xylenes, benzenes), ketones, esters, aliphatic compounds
Linoleum	*Aldehydes, carboxylic acid, aromatics (toluene)*
Solvent-based varnishes	Esters, aromatics (toluene, xylenes, benzenes), alcohols
Furniture, furniture varnishes	*Siloxanes, formaldehydes, among others*
Softwood	*Terpenes (pinenes, carenes, limonenes), formaldehyde*
Natural varnishes	Terpenes (pinenes, carenes, limonenes), aldehydes, aliphatic compounds
PVC flooring	Alcohols, softeners (2-ethylhexanol), vinyl chloride, organotin compounds
Polystyrene	*Aromatics (styrene)*
Wallpapers	*Ketones, aromatics (toluene), aliphatic compounds, formaldehydes*
Carpet flooring	Aromatics (styrene, toluene), amines, plasticizers
Water-based varnishes	Glycols, ketones, aldehydes, esters
Tobacco smoke	*Such as: aromatics, amines, ketones, formaldehydes*

Product, source	Semivolatile organic compounds possibly found in
Car interiors	Plasticizers
Caulking	PCB
Wood	Pesticides (wood preservatives), PAH
Protective wood finishes	Pesticides
Insecticide sprays	Insecticides (permethrin)
Fireplaces	PAH
Adhesives, varnishes	Plasticizers, flame retardants
Synthetic leather	Plasticizers
Synthetic products, general	Plasticizers, flame retardants
Leather (clothing, furniture)	Pesticides, azo dyes, chromium (VI)
Mattresses	Flame retardants, pesticides, plasticizers
Furniture	Flame retardants
Expanding foams	Flame retardants
Fluorescent lamps (old)	PCB in ballasts (until ca. 1989)
PVC flooring	Plasticizers, organotin compounds
Parquet sealant (old)	PCB
Parquet adhesives (old)	PAH (contaminated with PCB)
Sound insulation panels	PCB (until ca. 1978), flame retardants
Tobacco smoke	PAH (pesticides), among others
Wallpaper, textiles	Flame retardants
Wallpaper, vinyl	Plasticizers
Carpets, synthetic	Plasticizers, flame retardants
Carpets, wool	Pesticides (plasticizers)
Animal oil products	Pesticides, (plasticizers)
Textiles (clothing, furniture)	Pesticides, azo dyes

Figure 18
Occurrence of molds (M), yeasts (Y), and bacteria

Primarily found in	Type of microorganism
Air-conditioning systems, ventilation systems, air-conditioning units, and air filter systems	M
Grain mills	M
Nuts	M
Carpets, wallpapers, textiles, upholstery, mattresses	M
Stamp gumming adhesive, money	M
Air	M frequent, Y very rare
Dust, vacuum cleaners, vacuum cleaner bags	M frequent, Y very rare
Moisture damage, mold growth, mildew	M frequent, Y very rare
Indoor plants, gardening soil, and hydroponics	M frequent, Y rare
Sinks, work surfaces, sponges, cutting boards	M and Y
Food preparation areas, storage containers, bread boxes	M and Y
Kitchen appliances, sprouting equipment	M and Y
Vegetables, fruit	M and Y
Meat, sausage, cheese, specialty counters (open counters)	M and Y
Drains in kitchens, laundry rooms, bathrooms, siphons	M and Y
Showers, shower heads, bathtubs, silicone caulking	M and Y
Pets, aquariums, terrariums, pigeon feces	M and Y
Waste, compost, organic waste, plastic waste	M and Y, often also bacteria
Air humidifiers, air purifier	M and Y, often also bacteria
Water filters, water faucet adapters	M and Y, often also bacteria
Refrigerators, freezers, washing machines, dishwashers	M less common, Y frequent
Bathrooms, toilets, bidets, all sanitary areas	M less common, Y frequent
Dairy products	M less common, Y frequent
Juicers, yogurt makers, cereal bowls	Y
Toilet water, inside flushing cistern	Y
Toothbrushes, water picks, pacifiers, prostheses	Y
Drinking water, baby bottles, thermos jugs	Y

Toxicology

Many of these harmful substances are classified as teratogenic, embryotoxic, mutagenic, or carcinogenic (see Figures 19–20). In addition to sick building syndrome (SBS), which initially emerged in the first air-conditioned buildings in the 1970s, other disorders such as multiple chemical sensitivity (MCS) and chronic fatigue syndrome (CFS) occur more and more often. The increase in exposure levels may also be contributing to the incidence of burnout, electromagnetic hypersensitivity, nervous system diseases, or cancer. Many of the harmful substances do not cause immediate or acute health symptoms; instead, they gradually lead to self-poisoning. The accumulation of numerous different harmful substances ultimately creates a mix that, according to building biology, is beyond control and can break the proverbial camel's back.

Exposure Limits

Regarding indoor air pollutants, it is therefore virtually impossible to set safe limits for individual substances. Though there are official exposure limits in place to protect humans and the environment, they only limit major risks. Official exposure limits generally apply to industrial and commercial facilities. In Germany, for example, the following guidelines are in force: the Technical Instructions on Air Quality Control (TA Luft), or occupational health and safety limits (AGW and BGW) according to the Technical Rules for Hazardous Substances (TRGS), or the GISCODE product groups of the Hazardous Substances Information System by the building industry's accident prevention and insurance association (BG Bau), as well as product certification systems (EMICODE, Decopaint, and Blue Angel).

In 2007, the European Union regulation concerning the Registration, Evaluation, Authorisation and Restriction of Chemicals (REACH) came into effect. Manufacturers and importers are now obligated to list all chemicals that exceed a certain quantity (one metric ton per year) and all polymers that exceed a certain concentration level in products produced in or imported to the EU.[27] Even though these hazardous substances should be listed in the technical specifications and safety data sheets, a full declaration of ingredients or a laboratory analysis are often the only way to establish the absence of such a substance and thereby to eliminate any risks.

For additional support with product selection and testing, building biology consultants and testing specialists can be consulted, especially since legal regulations for limiting exposure to hazardous substances are often not adequate, in particular regarding residential housing. In close cooperation with the Institute of Building Biology and Sustainability IBN and in an interdisciplinary fashion, Baubiologie Maes developed the Standard of Building Biology Testing Methods (SBM),[28] which standardizes environmental testing and evaluation of indoor environments. The SBM covers risk factors in sleeping and living areas as well as on properties, specifying the basic facts, occurrences, and effects of indoor pollutants (with regard to recuperation and sleep), as well as building biology testing methods and remediation recommendations. It is divided into three main categories: fields, waves, radiation (physical agents); indoor toxins, pollutants, indoor climate (chemical agents); and fungi, bacteria, allergens (biological agents). The SBM serves as the basis of building biology testing and follows the premise: Any risk reduction is worth aiming at. Guideline values are meant as a guide. Nature is the ultimate standard.

Figure 19
Effects of volatile organic compounds

Volatile organic compounds	Common symptoms and possible health effects
Aromatic solvents	Carcinogenic, damage to the nervous system, premature births and miscarriages, sterility, fatigue, headaches, feeling of faintness, impaired balance and concentration
Aliphatic and olefinic solvents, terpenes, alcohols, ketones, esters, and siloxanes	Irritation of the mucous membranes, nausea, lung damage, fatigue, headaches, sensitization, multiple chemical sensitivity (MCS)
Chlorinated solvents	Nerve damage, accumulation in fatty tissue, fatigue, headaches, irritation of the mucous membranes, weakening of the immune system, fertility disorders
Glycol compounds	Malformations, increased infant deaths, damage to reproductive organs
Aldehydes (formaldehyde, furfural)	Suspected carcinogenic potential, irritation of the mucous membranes, burning eyes, hair loss, respiratory illnesses, allergies, headaches, irritability
Isocyanates	Irritation of the mucous membranes, damage to the eyes, damage to the upper respiratory tracts and alveoli, asthma, chronic illnesses

Figure 20
Effects of semivolatile organic compounds

Semivolatile organic compounds	Common symptoms and possible health effects
Pesticides – wood preservatives/PCP, lindane	Numbness, joint pains, fatigue, headaches, feeling of faintness, chloracne, skin and mucous membrane irritations, leukemia, liver damage, carcinogenic in animal testing, impaired nervous system function
Pyrethroids	Skin irritations, cramping, impaired concentration, impaired nervous system function
Plasticizers, phthalates	Accumulation in fatty tissues, fatigue, headaches, irritation of the mucous membranes, fertility disorders, impaired nervous system
Flame retardants – chlorinated phosphorus compounds	Allergic effects, increased susceptibility to infections, mutagenic effects, fatigue, impaired nervous system, irritation of the mucous membranes
PCB – polychlorinated biphenyls	Weakened or impaired immune system, fatigue, head and joint pain, chloracne, liver and kidney damage, weight loss, edema
PAH – polycyclic aromatic hydrocarbons	Clearly carcinogenic, liver and kidney damage

Spatial Theory[29]

The holistic concept of building biology also includes the impact space has at an emotional, mental, and spiritual level, because there is a causal link between sensory stimulation and the quality of life. With regard to color, shape, and proportions, well-designed spaces have a harmonizing effect on the occupants. Building Biology Interior Decorators IBN increasingly work with harmonic measures.

Figure 21
Proportions and their psychological effects

1	10:10/5:5/1:1	Firm
2	8:10/4:5	Downcast
3	3:5/5:8	Calm
4	5:10/1:2	Powerful
5	2:8/1:4	Intellectual

Scale and Shape

The use of artistic and architectural design makes it possible to experience space. In building biology, different design practices are used—preferably inspired by nature—to dimension and shape a given space, to open it up to daylight, and to include colors, tones, and sounds. Design practices are based on ancient laws of harmony found in, among others, feng shui, anthroposophy (living, organic patterns, but no geometric repetitions), or bionic architecture (based on the natural shapes of fauna and flora, e.g. logarithmic spirals), which also follow the laws of nature for their formal designs. Furthermore, building biology incorporates systems of measurement that are based on patterns of proportion that often occur in nature. Thus the canon of numbers that reveals itself, for example, in the golden ratio, the Modulor, and the mandalas, is also based on the laws of harmony.

Colors

As an intrinsic element of light, colors influence humans through their vibrations at an emotional, mental, and physical level too. Architectural psychology makes use of this connection. Colors are often associated with generally accepted effects. For example, the temperature of a room painted in a green-blue is often perceived as being 3 °C cooler than one painted in an orange hue. Complementary colors are also generally perceived in opposite ways (Figure 22). The effect of color on humans is dependent on their mental and physical condition as well as their age and gender. In building biology, subtle colors and natural tones are preferred and, in living and work environments, sharp contrasts or loud colors are used only sparingly or not at all (Figure 23).

Figure 22
Colors and their complementary effects

Color	Effect		Color	Effect
Yellow	Light	← →	Violet	Heavy
Orange	Warm	← →	Blue	Cold
Red	Stimulating	← →	Green	Calming
Purple	Serious	← →	Green-yellow	Cheerful

Figure 23
Colors and their effects by association

Color	Association (examples)	Negative effect
Blue	Yearning, infinity, depth	Loss of reality
Green	Peace, hope, life	Greed
Yellow	Friendliness, mind, thoughts	Envy
Orange	Joy, sensuality, self-confidence	Chaos
Red	Passion, energy, vibrancy	Aggression
Violet	Spirituality, solemnity, mysticism	
Purple	Power, splendor, dignity	
White	Clarity, openness, purity	
Black	Grief, darkness, withdrawal	
Gray	Melancholy, monotony, dispair	
Brown	Safety, dryness, narrowness	

Odors[30]

Odors also have a sensual dimension. They affect us subconsciously, trigger memories, and influence our moods. Bad odors annoy and irritate us, while pleasant scents raise our spirits—as do agreeable colors and hues. Hence rooms and their furnishings should have a pleasant or neutral odor.

Formative Value[31]

Handcrafted furniture made of natural materials usually imparts a pleasant odor. It also shapes the personal character of the user by conveying a sense of continuity, peace, and safety, as well as a feel for design, value, and quality. The respectful handling of the materials and the creative culture within the building biology community of craftspeople give it an additional formative value.

References

1 Prof. Dr. Anton Schneider, Building Biology Online Course IBN, Course Module: Introduction to Building Biology, Chapter 3.
2 Ibid.
3 As stated by Hans Carl von Carlowitz (1645–1714), the chief mining administrator of Freiberg, Saxony, in his work Sylvicultura Oeconomica from 1713.
4 Commission of Inquiry of the 12th German Bundestag, 26 June 1998.
5 Building Biology Online Course IBN (see Footnote 1), Chapter 7.
6 www.nachhaltigesbauen.de/nachhaltiges-bauen/nachhaltiges-bauen.html (accessed on 23 March 2017).
7 Building Biology Online Course IBN (see Footnote 1), Chapter 3.
8 Ibid.
9 Christoph Bijok, StadtLandschaften [UrbanScapes], Rosenheim: IBN-Verlag, 2015.
10 www.baubiologie.de/weiterbildung/25-grundregeln-der-baubiologie or www.buildingbiology.com/principles-of-baubiologie (accessed on 23 February 2017).
11 www.baubiologie.de/sbm or www.buildingbiology.com/about-the-institute (accessed on 23 February 2017).
12 Winfried Schneider/Wolf-Dieter Blank, Building Biology Online Course IBN, Course Module: Natural Building Methods.
13 E.g. Section 3 of the North Rhine-Westphalia Building Code (Landesbauordnung NRW).
14 Statement of the Dachverband Lehm e. V. from 26 September 2012, see dachverband-lehm.de or www.earthbuilding.info (accessed on 28 March 2017).
15 "Bauen mit Holz – Wege in die Zukunft", Hermann Kaufmann/Winfried Nerdinger (editors), commissioned by Architectural Museum of TU Munich and Professorship of Architectural Design and Timber Construction TU Munich, Prestel Verlag, Munich et al., 2012, p.17.
16 Winfried Schneider/Frank Hartmann/Ulrich Bauer/Dirk Dittmar, Building Biology Online Course IBN, Course Module: Energy-efficient Building Design.
17 Prof. Dr. Anton Schneider, Building Biology Online Course IBN, Course Module: Indoor Climate.
18 Winfried Schneider/Frank Hartmann, Building Biology Online Course IBN, Course Module: Heating and Ventilation.
19 Ibid.
20 Winfried Schneider/Frank Hartmann, Building Biology Online Course IBN, Course Module: Plumbing Systems and Water-efficient Strategies.
21 www.welt.de/wirtschaft/article8166646/Wasser-bleibt-eine-ungleich-verteilte-Ressource.html (accessed on 10 January 2017).
22 Prof. Dr. Anton Schneider, Building Biology Online Course IBN, Course Module: Electromagnetic Radiation;
   Dr. Thomas Haumann/Frank Hartmann, Building Biology Online Course IBN, Course Module: Electrical Wiring.
23 World Health Organization (WHO/IARC) 2011 in BioInitiative Report 2012, Summary for the Public, p. 5.
24 World Health Organization (WHO/IARC) 2011, Ibid.
25 Statistisches Bundesamt (Destatis.de), 2017, Privathaushalte: Energieverbrauch 2015 [Private Households: Energy Consumption 2015] (accessed on 23.03.2017).
26 Dr. Thomas Haumann, Building Biology Online Course IBN, Course Module: Air and Air Pollutants;
   Winfried Schneider/Wolf-Dieter Blank, Building Biology Online Course IBN, Course Module: Environmental Performance and Ecolabels.
27 www.reach-clp-biozid-helpdesk.de/de/REACH/Inhalt-REACH/Texte/Artikel6.html (accessed on 21 March 2017).
28 www.baubiologie.de/sbm or www.buildingbiology.com/about-the-institute (accessed on 23 February 2017).
29 Wolf-Dieter Blank, Building Biology Online Course IBN, Course Module 16: Raum — Form — Maß [Space—Shape—Scale];
   Gyan-Jürgen Schneider/Heinz Steinmeyer/Winfried Schneider, Building Biology Online Course IBN, Course Module: Natural Colors and Finishes.
30 Prof. Dr. Anton Schneider, Building Biology Online Course IBN, Course Module 17: Wohnpsychologie [Architectural Psychology].
31 Prof. Dr. Anton / Winfried Schneider, Building Biology Online Course IBN, Course Module 21: Möblierung [Furniture and Furnishings].

Checklist for Building Materials

	A Natural building materials	B Thermal properties	C Moisture behavior / sorption	D Water vapor diffusion (μ)	E Harmful substances	F Odor	G Electrobiology	H Radioactivity	I Environmental issues	J Energy use	K Fire behavior	L Airborne sound insulation	M Structure-borne/impact sound insulation	N Long-term sustainability	O Price/performance ratio	Score
Raw materials (incl. reconstruction)																
1 Solid wood	3	2	3	2	3	3	2	3	3	3	2	2	1	3	3	2.5
2 Clay products (also plaster)	3	1	3	3	3	3	3	2	3	3	3	3	1	3	2	2.6
3 Brick products	2	2	2	3	2	3	3	2	2	1	3	3	1	2	2	2.2
4 Aerated concrete	2	3	1	3	2	3	3	3	2	2	3	2	1	2	2	2.3
5 Sand-lime bricks	2	1	1	3	3	3	3	3	2	2	3	3	0	3	2	2.3
6 Concrete	1	0	0	0	2	2	3	2	2	0	3	3	0	2	2	1.5
7 Reinforced concrete	1	0	0	0	2	2	1	2	1	0	2	3	0	2	2	1.2
Mortars, plasters																
8 Lime mortar and plaster	2	1	2	3	3	3	3	3	2	2	3	3	0	3	2	2.3
9 Cement mortar and plaster	1	1	1	2	3	2	3	2	2	2	3	3	0	3	2	2.0
10 Synthetic resin plaster	0	1	0	0	1	1	2	3	0	1	2	3	0	2	1	1.1
11 Light mortar and plaster (perlite)	1	2	2	2	3	3	3	3	2	1	3	2	1	2	2	2.1
Thermal insulation materials																
12 Spray foam, synthetic	0	3	0	1	1	0	0	3	0	1	0	0	2	1	0	0.8
13 Fiberglass and mineral wool	0	2	0	3	1	0	2	2	0	1	2	0	3	1	1	1.2
14 Sheep wool	2	2	2	3	2	2	2	2	2	2	3	1	0	2	1	1.9
15 Flax, hemp	3	2	2	3	3	3	3	3	3	3	1	0	1	2	2	2.3
16 Cellulose	1	2	2	3	2	3	3	3	2	3	2	1	2	2	2	2.2
17 Low-density fiberboard	2	2	3	3	2	3	3	3	1	1	2	2	2	3	2	2.4
18 Cork	3	2	2	3	3	2	3	3	2	2	1	1	2	3	2	2.3
19 Coconut fiber	2	2	2	3	3	3	3	3	2	2	1	1	3	3	2	2.3
20 Loose-fill perlite	2	2	1	3	2	2	3	3	1	2	3	1	2	2	2	2.0
21 Wood wool board (magnesite-bound)	1	1	3	3	3	3	3	3	2	1	2	1	2	3	2	2.3

Assessment scores

0 – Significant shortcomings = Do not use
1 – Shortcomings = Not recommended
2 – Minor shortcomings = Recommended
3 – No shortcomings = Highly recommended

Material

Buiding materials – Notes

1 Without surface treatment and without adhesives
2 With or without natural fillers such as straw, jute, or perlite
3 Making it porous by adding wood chips, without fillers elevated radiation
4 70% sand, 15% lime, 10% cement, 2% gypsum
6 Sometimes questionable fillers
11 Light plaster with organic fillers (= polystyrene) also commercially available
14 Sheep wool, in some cases impregnated with toxicologically problematic urea derivatives
17 Some low-density fiberboards contain PU adhesives (isocyanate issues)
26 Bonded with adhesives up to 6% to 10% formaldehyde and/or isocyanates
28 Several veneer layers laminated, with phenolic resin-based adhesives

29 Isocyanate issues
31 Gypsum from flue gas desulfurization units at coal-fired power plants. No negative effects are known to date
32 Without artificial solvents and additives
33 Some products release toxins into the air
34 Some products release toxins into the air
35 Without emulsion film (synthetic resins, PVC), bonded with natural adhesives; backing layer made of jute fabric, a pronounced odor is discernible throughout the early months
36 PVC = polyvinyl chloride (chlorine, petroleum, additives such as plasticizers, stabilizers, flame retardants, heavy metal compounds)

Material	Natural building materials	Thermal properties	Moisture behavior / sorption	Water vapor diffusion (μ)	Harmful substances	Odor	Electrobiology	Radioactivity	Environmental issues	Energy use	Fire behavior	Airborne sound insulation	Structure-borne/impact sound insulation	Long-term sustainability	Price/performance ratio	Score
	A	B	C	D	E	F	G	H	I	J	K	L	M	N	O	
Vapor retarders/barriers																
22 Paper, PE-coated	1	–	2	2	2	2	2	3	1	2	1	–	–	1	2	1.8
23 PE foil	0	–	0	0	2	2	1	3	1	1	1	–	–	2	1	1.2
24 Aluminum foil	0	–	0	0	3	3	0	3	1	0	3	–	–	3	2	1.5
25 Bitumen felt	1	–	0	0	0	0	3	3	1	1	1	–	–	2	2	1.2
Sheathing boards																
26 Particleboards (resin-bound)	1	2	1	1	0	1	3	3	1	2	1	2	1	2	1	1.5
27 Particleboards (cement-bound)	2	1	1	2	3	3	3	3	2	2	2	3	0	3	2	2.1
28 Plywood	1	2	1	1	1	1	3	3	1	0	1	2	1	2	1	1.4
29 OSB boards	1	2	1	0	1	2	3	3	1	1	1	2	1	2	2	1.5
30 Natural gypsum boards	2	2	2	3	2	2	3	2	2	2	3	3	1	3	2	2.3
31 Synthetic gypsum boards (FGD)	1	2	2	3	2	2	3	2	2	2	3	3	1	3	2	2.2
Surface treatments/adhesives																
32 Natural resin products	2	–	2	2	2	2	3	3	2	2	2	–	–	2	2	2.2
33 Synthetic resin products	0	–	0	0	1	1	0	3	0	0	0	–	–	1	0	0.5
Miscellaneous																
34 Linoleum	2	2	1	0	2	1	3	3	2	1	2	2	2	2	2	1.8
35 PVC products (hard)	0	1	0	0	0	0	0	3	0	0	0	2	0	2	0	0.5
36 Glass	2	0	0	0	3	3	3	3	1	0	3	3	0	3	2	1.7

Assessment criteria

A Scores based on the degree of processing and other additives
B Heat conduction, heat storage, surface temperature
F Pleasant/unpleasant, neutral, unnatural, cold (in the medium term)
G Electrostatic buildup, electric conductivity, shielding of RF radiation
I Referring to availability (in the long term), manufacture, transport, processing and finishing, waste disposal
J During manufacture, processing and finishing, disposal, transport

K Assessment also in terms of toxic emissions in the case of fire
M Building materials 12, 13, 14, 17, 18, 19 are also available and used as insulation materials for impact sound. For the building materials 15 and 16, the assessment refers to their suitability as cavity insulation.
Without additional measures, perlite (20) is not suitable for use as impact sound insulation, but, in comparison to more rigid building materials, its impact sound properties are relatively good due to its elastic modulus.

The new IBN building serves as the flagship project and research facility of building biology and as an example of the commitment of the IBN to healthy and sustainable building practices.

The Flagship Project
of Building Biology

The New Building of the Institute of Building Biology + Sustainability IBN Rosenheim

As early as the 1970s, Anton Schneider, professor of wood biology, wood physics, and material testing, was preoccupied with building biology. His considerations always revolved around a holistic integration of humans, nature, and architecture. He began to train Building Biology Consultants IBN and to spread the teachings of healthy building through the Building Biology Correspondence Course IBN from 1977 and the IBN Sustainable Building and Living Magazine Wohnung + Gesundheit from 1979.

After an interdisciplinary collaboration with experts in other fields, Schneider published the 25 Principles of Building Biology in 1980, which are still valid today. In 1983, the Institut für Baubiologie + Ökologie Neubeuern IBN, which is now known as the Institute of Building Biology + Sustainability IBN, was established. Ever since, the IBN has closely cooperated with IBN-certified Building Biology Consulting Offices to provide both homeowners and building experts with answers to their questions regarding building biology and healthy building. The development of the Standard der Baubiologischen Messtechnik SBM (Standard of Building Biology Testing Methods SBM) in 1992 provided the basis for the training and activity of the Baubiologischen Messtechniker IBN (Building Biology Testing Specialists IBN), who offer assessments for building sites and homes.

The New Building

In 2014, under the management of Winfried Schneider, the Institute of Building Biology + Sustainability IBN decided to build a new institute in Rosenheim in strict accordance with building biology criteria. The project was designed by the IBN in collaboration with the architectural office of Martin Schaub, and it serves as the flagship building and research facility of building biology and as an example of the commitment of the IBN to healthy and sustainable building practices. Thus the building is not a completely new structure. Instead, the decision was made to use resources wisely and fully renovate a former grocery store in a housing complex built in the 1950s (Figure 1–3). By adding another floor, it was possible to have an exhibition space, administration area, and model residential unit all under one roof. This reconstruction effort preserves the mixed-use character of the area, provides good access to local services, and further enhances the neighborhood by upgrading and repairing the landscape design of the adjoining public green space. It was then possible to avoid sealing more ground surface and to create more green spaces instead.

The newly added two-level entrance foyer gives the building a welcoming appeal and completes the urban development. It offers ample space to invite visitors in and provides access to the residential unit and exhibition space on the ground floor, as well as to the office space on the upper floor via the open staircase (Figure 4).

Before construction began, the site and the existing building were assessed according to the Standard of Building Biology Testing Methods. The risks identified were taken into account and minimized during the design process. Elevated exposure levels were addressed and, with the consent of the neighbors, the asbestos cement siding of the neighboring building was replaced with a mineral-based external thermal insulation composite system.

Building Design

The two-level structure of the IBN building was designed to use a mix of construction types. A lightweight wood-frame structure was built on top of the existing masonry structure. The masonry on the ground level was renovated and fitted with additional sound and thermal insulation as required (Figure 5). For ecological reasons, the new entrance hall was completed as a heavy timber post-and-beam structure placed on a foundation of hollow concrete blocks whose environmental performance is considerably better than that of reinforced concrete (Figure 6). Those parts of the structure in contact with the ground were insulated with foam glass, as recommended in building biology. After the old roof had been dismantled, a glue-free dowel-laminated timber ceiling was anchored to a ring beam (Figure 7). The distortion of the Earth's magnetic field caused by the steel reinforcement could be reduced by around 90% through a demagnetization procedure. The soffit of the dowel-laminated timber ceiling is self-finished and features linear grooves to improve the acoustics of the room and its sound-absorbing properties. Furthermore, crushed limestone and natural fiberboards were installed on top of the ceiling for additional airborne and structure-borne sound insulation.

The wood-frame construction on the upper level was completed with prefabricated wall elements, which, in line with the planning objectives, were reinforced without the use of adhesive-bonded wood products (Figure 8). Blown-in wood fiber insulation was used here because it only requires a low amount of primary energy, and this layer was finished on the exterior with vapor-permeable natural fiberboard sheathing (Figure 9). On the ground level, the external thermal insulation composite system is also finished with vapor-permeable mineral-based plasters and silicate-based paints to satisfy the requirements of building biology.

The new IBN building serves as the flagship project and research facility of building biology and as an example of the commitment of the IBN to healthy and sustainable building practices.

On the upper level, the wood siding is made of spruce (Figure 10). The roof of the new top floor is a mono-pitched structure with a double layer of rafters that allows the roof overhang to be more slender. The top layer of the rafters is fitted with wood fiber insulation boards and the bottom layer is filled with blown-in insulation (Figure 11). Stainless steel roofing panels with double seams complete the roof construction.

Interior Materials

To create a comfortable indoor climate, nontoxic, renewable materials such as lime and clay were chosen for finishing the interior surfaces (Figure 12–13). This is part of the ongoing IBN research to gain insights into the processing qualities, aesthetics, and indoor climate impacts of different materials, as well as their cost. The wet rooms and selected masonry walls were completed with lime-based plaster and lime paints and in the splash water areas also with tiles (Figure 14). For flooring, solid wood parquets with different oil-based finishes were chosen to test their visual appearance, care requirements, and wear resistance. The built-in cabinets feature nontoxic linoleum on the exterior surfaces. To avoid exposure to volatile air pollutants, all handcrafted furniture was made from solid wood or white glue-bonded cross-laminated timber panels (three layers of dimensional lumber) and finished with natural resin-based oil or wax finishes. The doors and windows (Passive House standard) were also made of solid wood with a natural hard oil finish (Figure 15).

Lighting Design

The lighting design of the IBN building takes full advantage of maximum daylight exposure. As a result, the windows—whose dimensions follow the harmonic scale of the golden ratio—reach from the floor to almost as high as the ceiling on the ground level and run as a continuous band around the offices on the upper level. The office spaces feature external blinds with light control for sun and glare protection (Figure 16).

The artificial light was chosen to match the quality of natural daylight and designed with scenographic effects in mind. The halogen and LED lamps used have the lowest flicker rates possible and are dimmable. As a result, the intensity and color temperature of the light sources can be adjusted individually. In addition to the shielded task lamps at each workstation, indirect lighting illuminates various surfaces throughout the office space, thereby creating an overall balance of light and atmosphere of visual comfort (Figure 17).

Ventilation Strategy

To scientifically monitor the ventilation performance of the building and carry out on-site measurements, different ventilation zones with separate ventilation systems were developed. There are three ventilation zones according to use: the residential unit, the exhibition space, and the office floor. Each of these systems uses heat recovery and humidity regulation. Important features include: sufficient access openings for maintenance and cleaning, filtration for fine particulate matter, and duct silencers between the various zones of use. The demand-based control system adjusts air flow rates automatically, although manual override is possible at any time. The control parameters include threshold levels of carbon dioxide, relative air humidity ($< 50\%$), and room temperature, all of which are gathered by indoor air quality sensors. When natural ventilation is used, the ventilation system in the respective zone will reduce its flow rate and switch to basic operation mode. All windows were located in such a way as to allow for cross ventilation.

For different uses, different user profiles were defined: the user profile of the residential unit offers the highest level of indoor air quality and is suitable for allergy sufferers; the user profile of the exhibition space, where presentations are given and consultations provided, is defined as a meeting area, and the user profile of the office floor is based on the number of employees present during normal office hours. During events in the exhibition space, the ventilation system is supported by additional cross ventilation through windows, including the entrance foyer. Sources of hazardous emissions such as printers and photocopiers are placed closest to the exhaust air outlet so that employees are not exposed to their emissions.

It is the goal of the ongoing monitoring of these systems to research how and to what extent ventilation systems can be used over longer periods of time to meet building biology criteria and to determine their suitability. To this end, certain components of the system can be replaced such as alternative duct materials (e.g. wood or glass) or equipment parts (e.g. heat exchanger) to study their effects. Humidity recovery, in particular, is

1 Grocery store with public space
2 Grocery store prior to reconstruction in 2013
3 Preserved masonry walls of grocery store
4 The glass structure serves as both an entrance and a sun-room with a temperate temperature to buffer heat loss.
5 Existing masonry walls retrofitted with thermally insulating "Planziegel" clay blocks without fill
6 The frost wall made of hollow concrete blocks offers a much better environmental performance than reinforced concrete.

7 The dowel-laminated timber ceiling does not use any adhesives for bonding.

8 Diagonal sheathing acts as structural bracing for both the ceiling and the wall elements.

9 The wet-process wood fiber insulation boards have no isocyanate-based bonding agents added.

10 Through pretreatment, the graying of the wood siding due to the natural weathering process will be much more uniform.

11 For additional strength, the roof is fitted with diagonal sheathing.

12 Base coat clay plaster

13 Clay plaster on clay and wood fiber insulation boards

14 In the bathroom, the lime plaster is applied to reed boards.

15 For the insulation of the connection joints, hemp was used as a caulking material, but no spray foam sealant.

16 Even when the solar shading device is lowered, indirect, glare-free light can still be reflected deep into the room.

17

18

19

20

21

22

17 The light sculpture in the stairwell provides a welcoming appearance to the entrance foyer, even in the evening.

18 The hydronic heating pipes are embedded in plaster, which makes for a fast response time of the heating system.

19 The floor heating zones of the offices can be controlled individually.

20 To improve the poor shielding effectiveness of the wood-frame construction, an RF shielding mesh was integrated into the ventilated rainscreen of the wall assembly.

21 Roof-mounted photovoltaic system with an output of ca. 7,500 kWh

22 The plants and design elements using water and rocks were chosen to revitalize habitats for the urban flora and fauna.

Source
Viktoria Eva Maria Schuster, Bachelor's Thesis 06/2014
Nachhaltigkeitsbewertung (LCA und LCC) für den Teilneubau des Bürogebäudes IBN
[Sustainability Assessment (LCA and LCC) for New IBN Administration Building]
Figure 40: Comparison of the Impact Criteria between Variant 1 and Variant 2, p. 66
*Conventional building method using reinforced concrete with
external thermal insulation composite system (ETICS) and plastic glazing

Table 1
Environmental performance of the IBN building

			Variant 1 IBN	Variant 2*	Difference of V2 with V1
GWP	Global warming potential (climate change) kg CO$_2$	kg CO$_2$ e	-4,51	6,82	+ 251.21 %
AP	Acidification potential (dying forests and fish) kg SO$_2$	kg SO$_2$ e	0,023	0,039	+ 69.58 %
ODP	Ozone depletion potential kg R110	kg R11 e	-0,00000104	-0,000001	+ 3.80 %
POCD	Photochemical ozone creation potential kg C$_2$H$_4$	kg C$_2$H$_4$ e	0,00816	0,00984	+ 21.60 %
EP	Eutrophication potential (overfertilization) kg PO$_4$	kg PO$_4$ e	0,00553	0,00681	+ 23.15 %
PE nr	Primary energy nonrenewable	kWh	-5,75	14,37	+ 349.91 %
PE r	Primary energy renewable	kWh	92,75	72,13	- 22.23 %

a research focus. Microbiological testing will be carried out to document filter residues and the necessary maintenance and replacement cycles. To ensure correct operation, for example, an acoustic and a visual signal indicate when the filter needs to be replaced. The hygiene within the duct system is monitored via the access openings.

Heating Strategy

The low heating requirements of the highly insulated, airtight building are covered by low-temperature surface heating systems. The inlet temperature of 30 °C, and 35 °C at peak loads, combined with surface temperatures of 23 °C, is a reflection of the temperature range of the human body. Like the ventilation system, the central heating system is also divided into three zones: The residential unit is equipped with wall heating areas (Figure 18) and a floor heating system in the bathroom. The exhibition space and office floors are equipped with floor heating elements embedded in dry clay panels underneath the solid wood parquet flooring (Figure 19). The three heating zones operate independently of each other, but they all automatically compensate for the changes in weather and heating period. The heat-generating device runs on renewable resources, which are pellets in this case. The primary pellet furnace has an external air intake and the generated heat is transferred to a buffer tank, which is fitted with blown-in wood fiber insulation. All three heating zones are connected to the buffer tank separately. The furnace itself is visible from the exhibition space where it adds a sense of warmth and comfort like an enclosed fireplace; the heat output into the room can be reduced as needed.

Electrical Wiring Design

The goals of the electrical wiring design include a low-EMF installation and professional shielding against RF radiation. To accomplish these goals, halogen-free shielded wiring and receptacles, flicker-free lighting systems, and hardwired network and telephone technologies were chosen. An RF shielding mesh was installed to shield the wood-frame wall assembly (Figure 20). In contrast, the stainless steel roof, the exterior aluminum profiles of the wooden window frames, and the solid masonry walls on the ground level provide sufficient shielding against RF radiation. The RF shielding mesh on the walls of the upper floor and the stainless steel roof are connected to the main equipotential bonding bar and thus grounded. The power distribution and circuit breaker panels, server, and PV inverter are located in areas away from continuously occupied spaces. In keeping with the motto of the Standard of Building Biology Testing Methods (SBM) that "any risk reduction is worth aiming at," the exposure levels of ELF electric and magnetic fields as well as RF radiation were measured before and after completion. The final measurement results fell within the "no anomaly" range of the SBM and thus verify an electromagnetically clean indoor environment consistent with building biology recommendations.

The roof-mounted photovoltaic system covers a large part of the daily energy required by the offices (Figure 21). The payback period is estimated to be about ten years when taking the own consumption of electricity and the electricity supplied to the public power grid into account; mo-

nitoring is currently under way. No electric power storage was planned, but could be retrofitted. The low amount of electric power, which, for example, is needed for the on-demand tankless water heater in the residential unit, is supplied by a green power provider.

Water System

The decentralized hot water system optimizes hot water hygiene by reducing long stagnation periods in the pipes. Furthermore, in the IBN building, the last point-of-use faucet is chosen based on its frequency of use so that the entire in-house water distribution system is flushed daily. Between the main point of entry and the water distribution system, a test station was installed to be able to test different types of water treatment systems in the future. A rainwater collection system helps reduce the use of city water by supplying water to all points of use that do not require drinking water quality.

Outdoor Facilities

On the property, a newly created garden facing east adds more green space to the area and provides a welcome place of relaxation for users (Figure 22). In addition to removing areas of sealed asphalt pavement, the green roof on the garden shed and the integration of a buried rainwater drainage ditch support rainwater recovery and infiltration. As a result, it is unnecessary to drain the rainwater and snow melt into the public sewage system.

Conclusion

Due to the use of certified and renewable resources, the new IBN building scores high in sustainability assessments (LCA and LCC) based on the criteria of the German Sustainable Building Council (DGNB) (see Table 1). The use of vapor-permeable, hygroscopic, and natural materials promotes great indoor air quality as well as a great indoor climate and electroclimate, all of which create a healthy work environment. The integration of the IBN building into existing buildings enhances their value and promotes living together with the neighbors in intact natural surroundings. This makes the new IBN building a showcase project of building biology, especially since the 25 Principles of Building Biology[1] were applied here.

The newly created garden area provides a welcome place of relaxation for users.

Floor plans, scale 1:250

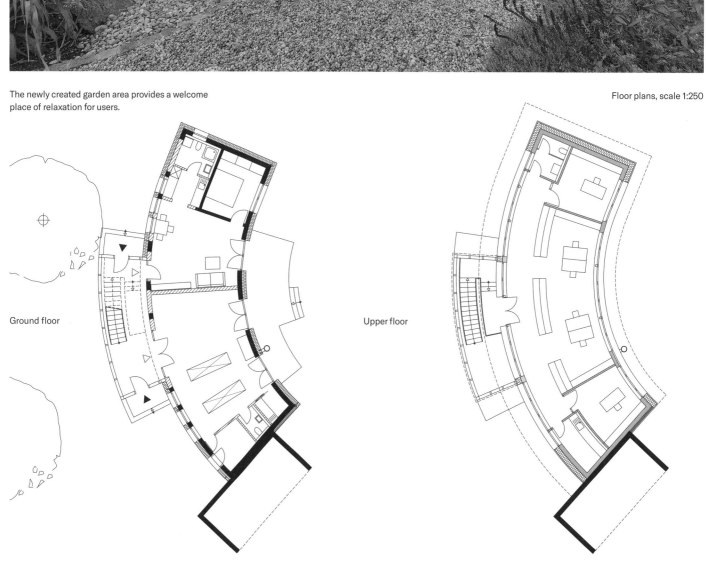

Ground floor

Upper floor

Scale 1:40

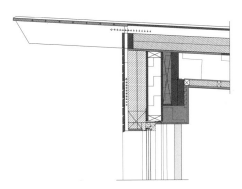

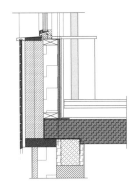

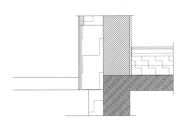

Roof
Roof U-value = ca. 0.09 W/m²K

Construction:
Clay finishing coat
Wood fiber insulation board 20 mm
Battens 40/60 mm with hemp insulation 60 mm
Vapor retarder, windproof
Bottom layer of rafters with
blown-in wood fiber insulation 280 mm
Solid wood sheathing 22 mm
Top rafters with wood fiber insulation boards 160 mm
Battens and ventilated rainscreen 80 mm
Solid wood sheathing 22 mm
Sarking membrane
Sound-deadening board
Stainless steel roof 0.5 mm with double standing seam

Wall construction upper floor
Exterior walls upper floor U-value = ca. 0.10 W/m²K

Construction:
Clay board 25 mm
Vapor retarder, moisture-dependent
Solid wood sheathing 20 mm
Wood-frame construction with
blown-in wood fiber insulation 160 mm
Low-density fiberboards 2 x 100 mm
Stainless steel shielding mesh
Battens and ventilated rainscreen 30 mm
Wood siding, spruce, T&G, pretreated

Wall construction ground floor / base
Exterior walls ground floor U-value = ca. 0.10 W/m²K

Construction:
Interior plaster: clay and lime plasters
Masonry: existing hollow concrete blocks 300 mm
New construction: Planziegel blocks without fill 300 mm
Ring beam interior and exterior insulated with cork 50 mm
External thermal insulation composite system with
blown-in wood fiber insulation 210 mm
Water-resistant low-density fiberboard exterior 50 mm
Base: foam glass boards 250 mm
Cement fiberboard, 10 mm on the outside as plaster base
Exterior plaster, mineral-based, finished with silicate paint

The Flagship Project of Building Biology

The newly added two-level entrance foyer
gives the building a welcoming
appeal and completes the urban development.

Project	New building of the Institute of Building Biology + Sustainability
Architect	IBN with the Architectural Office of Martin Schaub, Rosenheim
Client	Institute of Building Biology + Sustainability IBN
Location	Rosenheim, Germany
Completion	January 2015
Gross floor area	Usable area 250 m²
Construction cost	No information available
Efficiency standard/certification	Passive house/energy-plus house
Annual heating energy demand	20 kWh/m²a
Annual primary energy demand	64.3 kWh/m²a
U-value exterior wall	0.10 W/m²K
U-value roof	0.09 W/m²K

Endnote   1 Neues Institutsgebäude IBN–Teil 2 und die 25 Grundregeln der Baubiologie: baubiologie.de/downloads/wug/Volltextartikel/neues_ibn.pdf
                (accessed on 2 April 2017).
Sources   IBN publications: New Building for the Institute of Building Biology + Sustainability IBN,
                collection of articles from Wohnung + Gesundheit, 2013–2015
                neubauibn.baubiologie.de
                Marc Wilhelm Lennartz, "40 Jahre Baubiologie in Deutschland," Bausubstanz, 4, 2015

To avoid exposure to volatile air pollutants, all handcrafted furniture was made from solid wood or white glue-bonded cross-laminated timber panels (three layers of dimensional lumber) and finished with natural resin-based oil or wax finishes.

Twenty Examples
from a Building Biology Perspective

The entrance foyer offers ample space to invite visitors
in and provides access to the residential suite
and exhibition space on the ground floor as well as to
the office space on the upper floor via the open
staircase.

The historic half-timbered house in the well-preserved
part of the settlement of Niederhofheim in
Liederbach am Taunus is testament to the local
village structures still in evidence today.

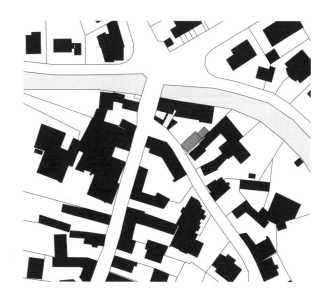

Site plan, scale 1:2000

Haingraben Half-Timbered House
Liederbach am Taunus, Germany

Designated as a historic property, this half-timbered house in the well-preserved part of the settlement of Niederhofheim in Liederbach am Taunus is testament to the local village structures still in evidence today with the collection of traditional L-shaped farmyards. The dendrochronological analysis of the beams dated the construction of the building to 1769. In the course of its long existence, the half-timbered house has undergone a number of renovations. The facade of the ground floor, for example, was changed from timber frame to masonry, and window sizes were also changed. In 2013, the Office of Architecture and Historic Preservation undertook complete renovation of the almost 250-year-old building. An annex—designed to current modern standards—was added in keeping with the basic concept, now housing all sanitary facilities. The local historic preservation authority was in favor of this solution, where the restrooms are placed in an annex to protect the historic timber-frame structure, and thus approved the annex.

By using primarily vapor-permeable and hygroscopic natural materials, the historic building was renovated in accordance with the principles of building biology and in line with the existing aesthetic features. On the inside, the timber-frame facade with clay brick infill was lined with reed insulation boards and finished with clay plaster and calcimine, while on the outside, the reed insulation boards had a lime plaster applied with a woven jute fabric and a colored lime finishing plaster. An insulating lime plaster and a lime paint were applied to

the masonry of the ground level, thereby setting the color of the facade of the upper level apart from the rest of the building. The reconstruction of the window distribution and alignment with custom-made wood-muntin windows gave the building its (new) old appearance. This allowed the building to be restored as closely as possible to its original state as documented in a family photo of the house when it was owned by the grandparents of the current residents. Throughout the seasons, the exterior folding wood shutters provide additional protection for the double-glazed and single-pane windows on the upper floor. As a result, the exterior walls meet the energy efficiency standard for historic properties stipulated by the German government-owned development bank KfW, the KfW Energy Efficiency House "Heritage," and this was achieved by meeting the principles of building biology and created a favorable indoor climate in the process. The renovation of the roof of the main building is also in keeping with the bygone style of the old structure and barely visible thanks to the reutilization of the aged plane tiles, which add to the value of the historic property. The conditions for the approval of a loan led to insulating the attic with rock wool (man-made mineral fiber or MMMF), precluding the planned use of wood fiber insulation boards. The walls of the room in the attic, which is occasionally used as a guest bedroom, are covered with humidity-regulating clay boards that have a positive impact on indoor climate due to their sorption capacity and for which a surface depth of only 20 to 30 mm is necessary.

The typical three zones of timber-frame construction were preserved on the inside. At the same time, it was possible to address the clients' desire for more modern facilities and openness in the floor plan by removing dead ends and maximizing the diffusion of light. This was realized with additional door openings from the peripheral zones to the middle of the house and by enlarging the stairwell on the upper floor. The formerly steep single-stringer staircase was replaced by a custom-made double-stringer spiral staircase. Now the open, delicate structure of the staircase visually connects the floors of the house as well as allowing more light to penetrate, creating the desired spatial generosity within the constraints of the timber-frame system.

The floor slab on the ground level was rebuilt to eliminate potential moisture problems historic half-timbered houses are notorious for. As is common practice in many other renovation projects completed by this architectural office, the newly sealed and insulated floor slab was fitted with a floor heating system to "squeeze out" any existing moisture. This follows the use of secondary or baseboard heating systems when working with historic masonry construction to help dry rising moisture in walls. The floors were laid with solid Douglas fir planks with a vapor-permeable finish, supporting a great indoor climate due to their humidity-regulating properties. The building is heated with radiant heat for exceptional thermal comfort and its positive effect on indoor air quality. The low-temperature heating system is powered by an energy-efficient condensing gas boiler, as are the heating panels

on the upper floors and the domestic hot water, whereby its volume is adjusted to meet the needs of the users. For safe drinking water, copper pipes were chosen to minimize the risk of the formation of a bacterial film. And a water softener unit was installed to keep the water within a pH range of 7.3-8.5, thus avoiding limescale buildup (which would increase the pumping energy requirement) and reducing the risk of increased amounts of copper being dissolved into the water. Galvanized copper pipes are another option to avoid contamination. The project was realized almost exclusively with regional craftspeople and thus strengthened the local economy. Not only the handcrafted joinery and carpentry work, but also the use of clay-based products, increase the value of the building both aesthetically and materially, making an important contribution to the appreciation of handcrafted solutions as a whole.

The floors were laid with solid Douglas fir planks
with a vapor-permeable finish, supporting a
great indoor climate due to their humidity-regulating
properties.

Project	Haingraben Half-Timbered House
Architect	Büro für Architektur und Denkmalpflege, Bastian Völler
Client	Private
Location	Liederbach, Germany
Completion	2014
Gross floor area	212 m²
Construction cost	370,000 EUR
Efficiency standard / certification	KfW Efficiency House "Heritage"
Annual heating energy demand	14,490 kWh/a – 68.35 kWh/m²a
Annual primary energy demand	18,507 kWh/a – 87.29 kWh/m²a
U-value exterior wall	Half-timbered 0.156 W/m²K – masonry 0.598 W/m²K
U-value roof	Half-timbered 0.156 W/m²K – masonry 0.598 W/m²K

Sources   architektur-denkmalpflege.net; architektur-denkmalpflege.net/architektur/2013/036_haingraben.html;
             Bastian Völler, short description

An annex—designed to current modern standards—
was added in keeping with the basic concept,
now housing all sanitary facilities.

Thus the building is heated with radiant heat
for exceptional thermal comfort and
its positive effect on indoor air quality.

Ground floor   Upper floor   Attic floor   Floor plans, scale 1:250

Their love for the traditional craft of carpentry and
an appreciation of the history of old buildings
drove the Heringer couple to carefully dismantle an old
peat barn in 2006 and then to reassemble it at a
new site to use it as their residence and workshop.

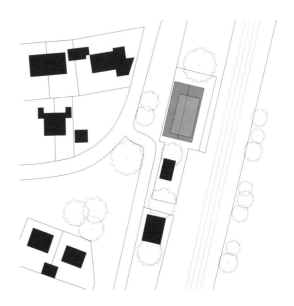

Site plan, scale 1:2000

Residence and Workshop in an Old Peat Barn
Schechen, Germany

Their love for the traditional craft of carpentry and appreciation of the history of old buildings drove the Heringer couple to carefully dismantle an old peat barn in 2006. They then made the necessary, handcrafted repairs and reassembled the barn at a new site, after finally finding an appropriate plot in 2012. The barn is used as a residence and workshop. The new location of the old peat barn is also characterized by a respectful treatment of the surrounding area and buildings. When the old train station grounds were rezoned, the master metal worker and wickerwork designer seized the opportunity to not only rebuild the peat barn, but also part of the village settlement area by locating their workshops in a previously unused building of the train station adjoining the barn. This resettlement also led to a continuation of the village structure, while at the same time giving it an urban[1] character. It allows the clients to live and work in a village setting, while still having a direct link to the public railroad network they use for their daily trips to Munich. The distinctly green character of the development area carries through here, allowing for a lifestyle close to nature.

With the support of the architects Roswag and engineers Ziegert | Seiler, the clients created a comprehensive ecological ensemble with a clear regional focus. All materials of the new components of the building were sourced locally. With a do-it-yourself approach, the help of local craftspeople from the surrounding areas, and the use of regional materials, it was possible to create a building made of wood and clay that features exceptional properties in terms of building biology.

The elongated barn building is ideally aligned along the length of the site. From north to south, the unheated spaces such as the storage and workshop areas are followed by the heated office spaces and living areas in that order. This results in the buffer spaces being zoned in accordance with the points of a compass. Once the peat barn had been rebuilt, a structure was set off-center within the old load-bearing frame of the barn according to the house-within-a-house principle. The new, heated structure juts out of the barn building line on the eastern side to capture the morning sun and create a recessed shady veranda to the west that serves as an outdoor extension of the living space, even during the shoulder seasons. The roof, too, sticks out of the existing roof surface and opens to the sky with glazing along the roof ridge. This allows daylight to enter the middle zone of the building through the glass ceiling to reach into the rooms on the ground floor.

The wood-frame construction of the new building features blown-in wood fiber insulation in combination with natural fiberboard sheathing. The environmental performance of natural fiberboards, which are made of renewable materials using wet processing without any adhesives, is excellent due to their low embodied energy requirements. The use of these sheathing boards in the roof and wall assemblies as bracing or plaster bases is therefore a great ecological choice. Both on the inside and the outside, the building features a clay base plaster with a clay finishing plaster, but without any additional coatings of paint. Thanks to the recessed wall areas facing the old building and the

projecting roof sections, clay could also be applied to the exterior wall of the new building, despite the material not being weather-resistant due to its sensitivity to water. Clay, which is available in more or less unlimited amounts in many parts of the world, is a highly regarded material in building biology because of its technical properties in building science terms. Not only the diffusion and sorption capacity, which define its ability to absorb humidity and pollutants, but also its excellent heat storage capacity make clay such a great all-round material. This is why clay walls are often thermally activated. The exterior walls of the new building, for example, were completed with in-wall heating. The wall that bisects the space on the upper level was built in wood-frame construction and filled with clay bricks to have heating pipes embedded in the plaster. The temperature control on the ground level is provided by an in-floor heating system between the loose crushed glass insulation on the new foundation below and the wood flooring above. To increase the available thermal mass, the interior walls of the ground floor were completed with clay bricks. All in all, a structure has been created that offers a healthy and balanced indoor climate, ensures comfortable surface temperatures, and provides a well-balanced ratio of thermal insulation to heat storage capacity. The high level of energy efficiency and the airtight installation of the building envelope make this new structure a nearly zero-energy building that illustrates the future viability of historic buildings and building biology-based practices.

The avoidance of hazardous substances also extends to the interior surface treatments. The visible wood surfaces were treated with natural nontoxic finishes. The wood of the existing building was finished with boiled linseed oil, while the fir planks of the flooring were soaped. In addition to the surfaces finished with clay finishing plasters and polished lime plasters, the white silicate-based paints used on the sloping roof walls and ceilings create bright, healthy living spaces.

The thorough ecological approach is also reflected in the choice of the mechanical, electrical, and plumbing systems. The heating energy is supplied by a log wood boiler powered with waste wood from the clients' own wickerwork workshop and forest on site. Furthermore, the system is also fed with renewable power from solar collectors via a stratified storage tank for domestic hot water and heating energy. The design team chose not to install a ventilation system after assessing the humidity-regulating and sorption properties of the interior plaster with a thickness of 20 to 30 mm. The combination of clay surface areas and manual cross ventilation was deemed sufficient by the users to meet the hygiene requirements for air exchange. The users' active involvement in the ventilation process is paramount here.

Once the peat barn had been rebuilt, a structure
was set off-center within the old load-bearing
frame of the barn according to the house-within-
a-house principle.

Project	Residence and Workshop in an Old Peat Barn
Architect	Ziegert I Roswag I Seiler
Client	Private
Location	Schechen, Germany
Completion	2014
Gross floor area	698 m², usable area: 259 m² heated, 229 m² unheated
Construction cost	350,000 EUR
Efficiency standard / certification	Nearly zero-energy building (EnEV 2009 -30%)
Annual heating energy demand	37.19 kWh/m²a
Annual primary energy demand	21.3 kWh/m²a
U-value exterior wall	0.13 W/m²K
U-value roof	0.15 W/m²K
Awards	Architektouren 2016
	Anerkennung geplant + ausgeführt 2016 [Acknowledgment]
	Lobende Erwähnung, HolzbauPlus 2016 [Honorary Mention]
	Sonderpreis Das Goldenen Haus 2016 [Special Award]
	Fritz Bender Award 2016

Endnotes   1 Cf. Christoph Bijok, StadtLandschaften, IBN-Verlag, 2015.
            2 Wolfgang Maes, Stress durch Strom und Strahlung, IBN-Verlag, 6th edition, 2013, p. 82.
            3 Ibid., p. 120 ff.
Sources   zrs-berlin.de
            ZRS press kit 10/2016
            Geflechtundraum.de/index.php/projekte/besondere-projekte/17
            Achim Pilz, Historische Torfremise, Wohnung + Gesundheit, 158, 3, 2016
            Friederike Meyer, Torfstadel Schechen, Bauwelt, 6, 2015

The proximity of railroad tracks to the project had to be looked at separately based on building biology recommendations regarding electromagnetic fields. Any leakage current, which is caused by poor isolation of the running rails, can spread magnetic fields across the conductive moist ground and underground metal piping and trans-mission lines in the vicinity.[2] Chronic exposure to ELF magnetic fields can lead to stress-related health problems.[3] Since the trains here are diesel-powered, the exposure to artificial fields can be more or less ruled out. What remains, however, are the issues of noise disturbance every half hour and air pollution from the diesel exhaust fumes.

Ground floor   Upper floor   Attic floor   Floor plans, scale 1:250

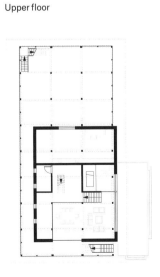

The architect Ingomar Reumiller renovated the stable part of the wood lodge in Andelsbuch by considering both the present and future needs of the family.

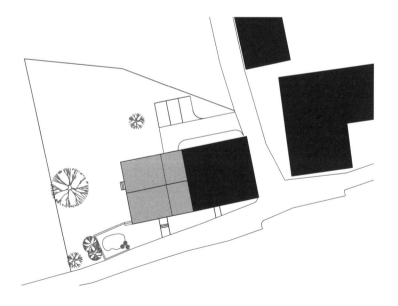

Site plan, scale 1:1000

Ritter-Reumiller House
Andelsbuch, Austria

In their search for a healthy living space, it was a stroke of luck that the Ritter-Reumiller family of five could resort to an existing building they already owned. For one thing, the 150-year-old barn, which had been used previously for the family's farming operation and housed a bakery, could be partially preserved and renovated. For another, the children could use the site with its large garden in the middle of the cultural landscape of the Bregenz forest for their own creative adventures close to nature. The architect Ingomar Reumiller renovated the stable part of the wood lodge in Andelsbuch by considering both the present and future needs of the family. A partial demolition of the stable was inevitable, but the new rear section of the proposed building and the front of the house formed an existing framework that was realized with great dedication. The new stable structure with its moderate temperature gives not only the children a chance of using this extended space for many different activities in a family, social, and cultural context. Also, owing to the ecological approach taken by the architect, the materials left over from the partial demolition were reused. The existing building serves as a storage space not only for firewood, but also for garden furniture and gardening tools. The newly arranged barn section was also refitted with siding boards and window frames. The new three-level rear building was rebuilt to project slightly beyond the roof line of the front building. It was completed without projecting roofs like those of the wood lodge, creating a monolithic house, but still with traditional features. The floor plan was designed to be suitable for family life and adaptable for future uses;

for example, the ground floor was conceived for potential separation and barrier-free use at a later stage. The upper level now houses a two-floor living and dining space that constitutes the center of family life. This space reaches to the ridge of the roof and faces the barn, establishing visual connections between the large, glass-clad area, the barn, and the airy space it creates. The skylights embedded in the roof amplify the sense of generous space and provide the living area facing southwest with maximum light and warmth from the sun. On both floors, the bedrooms are located to the north as thermal buffer rooms and face away from the access road outside to prevent noise pollution. The kitchen and the bathrooms, which require extra heat, are in the core areas.

The building design takes its cues from the principles of building biology with regard to healthy living and sustainability. The project was built mainly with renewable and natural building materials. Both the embodied energy used to extract and produce raw materials and their ease of dismantling and composting after use were considered. The load-bearing structure is made of solid timber, which consists of regional spruce and silver fir dimensional lumber laminated using hardwood dowels and no adhesives.

Furthermore, the entire thermal building envelope is very effectively insulated with ecologically responsible straw bales of up to 500 mm in thickness. This choice of ecologically responsible materials continues

This space reaches to the ridge of the roof and faces the barn, establishing visual connections between the large, glass-clad area, the barn, and the air space it creates. The skylights embedded in the roof amplify the sense of generous space and provide the living area facing southwest with maximum light and warmth from the sun.

on the inside with healthy clay applied to the post-and-beam walls insulated with wood fiber. Clay boards and clay plasters—ranging from fine to polished without any further surface treatment—were used to create balanced moisture conditions and, by extension, a healthy indoor climate. Polished and soaped lime surfaces in the bathroom and hallway areas also contribute to a healthy indoor climate, as does the rough-sawn wood strip flooring without transitions, which is oiled/waxed in the wet rooms. This means that the project was realized without the use of expanding foams, adhesives, paints, or the like.

The rhombus profile siding was completed using untreated spruce strips of varying widths. In keeping with regional building traditions, the siding was mounted vertically. And thanks to the direction of the openings—away from prevailing winds—the siding is protected from the weather and will last for a long time. The varying widths of the siding profiles, which are deliberately chosen, give the facade a subtle liveliness and naturalness that enhance its precise, symmetrical structure. In contrast to the traditional proportions of the region and owing to the relatively deep reveals, large-size, single-casement fixed glazing units in wooden frames made of spruce complete the appearance of the facade. These units are insulated with an additional layer of sheep wool and feature triple-glazed panels with windowsills made of sturdy oak.

As an additional heat source, natural radiant heat meets the remaining heating requirements of this nearly zero-energy building. The masonry heater made of rammed earth supplies heat from renewable energy sources to the entire building. The rammed-earth surface areas of the heater as well as the flooring areas act as radiant heat surfaces here. The floor heating system, which has a quick response time, was installed as a dry system, using clay, crushed stone, and wood fiber insulation. The additional support provided by the solar thermal collectors makes it possible to use the central heating system in summer too to supply the domestic hot water. To ensure safe drinking water, the water piping is made of stainless steel. Indoor air quality and hygiene are ensured by a controlled air intake and exhaust ventilation system with heat recovery. The ventilation system is mostly used in winter and was equipped with ground source heat pumps to condition the intake air. Besides the selection of materials, the craftspeople involved also add to the regional nature of the project. Most of the construction work was completed by local craftspeople from the Vorarlberg region and the homeowners themselves. The final result is remarkable in building biology terms: neighborhood living, close connection to nature, and the coexistence of living and working all rolled into one.

The house was completed without projecting roofs like those of the wood lodge, creating a monolithic building, but still with traditional features.

Project	Ritter-Reumiller House
Architect	Atelier für Architektur & Mehr, Ingomar Reumiller
Client	Private
Location	Andelsbuch, Austria
Completion	11/2010
Gross floor area	255 m², usable 171.3 m²
Construction cost	Information not available
Efficiency standard / certification	Nearly zero-energy house
Annual heating energy demand	17 kWh/m²a
Annual primary energy demand	Information not available
U-value exterior wall	0.11 W/m²K
U-value roof	0.09 W/m²K

Sources   i-reumiller.jimdo.com
Florian Aicher, Hermann Kaufmann, Belebte Substanz, Umgebaute Bauernhäuser im Bregenzerwald, Munich: DVA, 2015

Ground floor   Upper floor   Attic floor   Floor plan, scale 1:250

The straw bale house project by Georg Bechter
Architektur + Design is a house with a thick
outer shell, but a flexible core—a seemingly simple,
yet extraordinary project.

Site plan, scale 1:2000

Straw Bale House
Dornbirn, Austria

The straw bale house project by Georg Bechter Architektur + Design is a house with a thick outer shell, but a flexible core—a seemingly simple, yet unusual, extremely interesting project in terms of building biology. The one-level, single-family detached residence is composed almost entirely of natural building materials that are grown and readily available in the region. A bale of straw defines the shape and serves as the main building material. Besides being approved by German building authorities as a building material, the straw bales in this Austrian project at Dornbirn are also used for load-bearing purposes. Like bricks, the straw bales are stacked into exterior walls covered with a solid wood roof structure made of three-layer cross-laminated timber panels. The roof is also insulated with straw and, in addition, extensively planted with vegetation. Straw bales became the material of choice for the homeowners because they aligned the most with their requirements of a locally available, low-cost material with a good environmental performance that promotes the sense of a comfortable living space. Furthermore, the new home was to meet high ecological standards of quality, be an affordable living space, and allow for barrier-free use with advancing age.

This led to an open, flexible interior design concept that creates a "living landscape" once the modular furniture is added. Auxiliary functions are organized in their respective "housings" and integrated sliding panels make it possible to freely combine the spaces with one another. In addition, the thickness of the exterior walls allows for window alcoves: one integrates the bathtub and the other features a seating opportunity. The building complements the urban development of the local town. The new house lies at the edge of Dornbirn along the urban development boundary and acts as a link between the urban development area and the adjoining reed lands. With its natural charm, the building offers a harmonious transition into nature. As a salient feature of the exterior, the roof traces the clear, simple form of the building and at the same time protects the naturally soft straw bale walls with its reach. The exact lines of the spruce siding are inclined towards the glass facade and also provide a frame for the patio that extends along the entire front of the glazed structure. This inclined surface also serves as the patio roof, preventing solar overexposure in summer, yet allowing the warmth of the sun to reach deep into the building in winter. The uses of the interior spaces are aligned with the path of the sun across the sky. The bedroom areas are located to the east, while the living and dining room area is in the southwestern section of the house. This makes it possible to move through the use of the rooms throughout a given day and at the same time to maximize the use of daylight via the ceiling-high glazing along the patio side. The openings to the north are smaller, but provide visual connections to nature outside. Thus the building is beautifully awash with daylight despite the thick exterior walls.

According to the architect Georg Bechter, natural materials create an, "incredible aura and indoor climate in which one feels extremely comfortable."[1] The exterior straw bale walls were finished with clay plaster on the inside and lime plaster on the outside, which makes for a vapor-permeable and hygroscopic wall construction that naturally regulates indoor climate. This type of construction prevents the buildup of moisture in the straw and thus prevents mold growth too. Indoor climate also profits from the fact that all interior furnishings, including the ceiling, are made of wood without the use of any surface treatments. Furthermore, the uniform appearance affords a soothing spaciousness. The contrast between the angular wooden surfaces and the soft edges of the clay surfaces creates an appealing juxtaposition and highlights the craftsmanship of both. The high haptic quality of the interior surfaces is also evident in the polished screed floor finished with a silicate-based densifier.

When building with straw, structural requirements for a high-quality structure and professional installation should be taken into account. The 30 mm thick layer of plaster on both sides protects the straw from small animals and gives the structure an F30 fire resistance rating. Along the edges and across connection points, insect screening was installed. During the construction process, the connecting work was proceeded with only after allowing the completed structure to settle for four to six weeks, because straw bales continue to settle for some time. In this project, the straw bales settled by 120 to 200 mm. Fur-

thermore, the siding of the roof structure in the southern section integrated a ventilated rainscreen. As far as environmental performance is concerned, straw bales achieve an excellent result. As a regional by-product of grain cultivation, their production only requires a low amount of energy. In addition, they bind CO_2 and are ultimately compostable at the end of their life cycle.

The discernible simplicity of the architectural concept continues with the building technology. The 1200 mm wide straw bale exterior walls and the 700 mm thick straw bale roof insulation provide optimal thermal insulation. This and the solar benefits achievable during winter make it possible to reduce the required building technology to an absolute minimum. A simple tiled stove combined with the thermal mass of the activated screed floor and foundation slab supplies heating for the entire floor area. This is further combined with triple-glazed windows that can be opened for cross ventilation as needed. Overheating via the western side of the building during summer is prevented with retractable blinds mounted on the outside of the roof incline. In line with the conscious choice of a low-tech approach, there are only two more systems added: a decentralized domestic hot water system and a reduced home wiring system. The piping and wiring is mainly run in the floor slab, while the outlets are mainly located in the built-in furniture boxes.

As a salient feature of the exterior, the roof traces the
clear, simple form of the building and at the
same time protects the naturally soft straw bale walls
with its reach.

Project	Straw Bale House
Architect	Georg Bechter Architektur + Design
Client	Private
Location	Dornbirn, Austria
Completion	2014
Gross floor area	178 m², usable area 126 m²
Construction cost	Net: 300,000 EUR
Efficiency standard / certification	Information not available
Annual heating energy demand	26 kWh/m²a
Annual primary energy demand	Information not available
U-value exterior wall	0.04 W/m²K
U-value roof	0.06 W/m²K
Awards	ZV Bauherrenpreis 2016 [Clients' Award of Austrian Architects Association]

Endnote   1 Interview with Matthias Köb on breathe-aut.com (accessed on 03 March 2017)
Sources   bechter.eu; Georg Bechter Architektur + Design, Strohhaus Dornbirn. Dicke Schale, flexibler Kern, office publication
             Matthias Köb, Haus aus Stroh, breathe-aut.com
             Herbert Gruber, Lasttragendes Strohballenhaus in Dornbirn, baubiologie.at
             Detail Online – Kompostierbare Wände, Strohhaus, AIT, 1/2, 2015

This led to an open, flexible interior design concept that creates a "living landscape" once the modular furniture is added. Auxiliary functions are organized in their respective "housings" and integrated sliding panels make it possible to freely combine the spaces with one another.

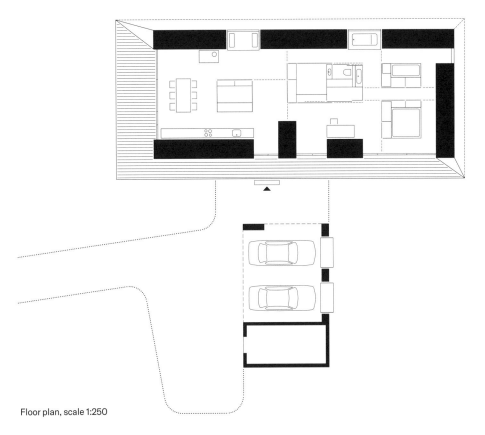

Floor plan, scale 1:250

To preserve the historic log structure
in its original state, a timber "insert" was integrated
into the existing structure.

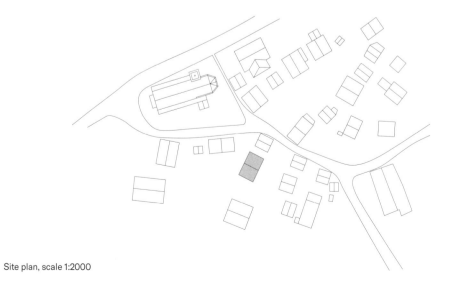

Site plan, scale 1:2000

Casa C
Reckingen, Switzerland

The village of Reckingen in an alpine valley of the Upper Valais region is characterized by the extremely well-preserved Swiss chalet architecture of heavy timber and log construction. Casa C also preserves its existing historic structure. The stable and barn building was built in 1890 and left vacant after the stable had been abandoned due to changes in animal protection regulations. In 2012, it was then renovated and refurbished based on plans by Camponovo Baumgartner Architekten to serve as Casa C. To preserve the historic log structure in its original state, a timber "insert" was integrated into the existing structure. The dual animal stable and hay storage system of the original layout was maintained so that the ground floor can serve as a storage area and mechanical floor, while the barn section was expanded to be used as a vacation home. The two sections of the previous layout are still strikingly evident as two sections of the inserted building are recessed. The two recessed balconies, which are staggered accordingly, feature generous floor-to-ceiling glazing that offers splendid views of the existing building and the local village. This design creates sheltered open spaces: one serves as the weather-protected entrance area, and the other—facing the living spaces—acts as a patio sheltered from the sun. At the same time, the existing openings of the old facade offer a wide variety of vistas. Casa C preserves the traditional architecture, while showing a way to reconstruct it in a modern and ecological manner.

The respect for traditional building methods and handcrafted solutions continues on the inside with the creative approach to the dual uses of the house. The new spatial design of the house required only two openings in the existing structure to implement the spiral alignment of the living spaces around the "middle wall." This created a sequence of different consecutive living spaces. A continuous flow leads the user from the entrance to the living and dining area (first opening), followed by the staircase that provides access to the bedrooms on the upper floor via a long living space (second opening), which spans the width of the two facades and reaches up to the roof ridge. These two air spaces also connect the floors vertically, thereby creating a sense of generous space and sharpening the contrast between old and new.

It was a fundamental premise of this project to use as many local materials as possible—particularly wood—to promote ecological building and support the local timber industry as well as skilled trades and crafts. The integrated post-and-beam structure was built with regionally available structural timber and the existing heavy timber structure was then repurposed to function as the siding of the new building. Reinforcement was added to the ground floor for structural reasons. The existing steel beams in one part of the ground floor ceiling have additional steel supports and, in another stable area, wood beams and new wood posts are used. Due to its magnetic properties, steel distorts the Earth's magnetic field. Steel elements can be demagnetized, as recommended in building biology. However, since there are no bedrooms above the steel beams of the ground floor, there is no

need to worry about any negative health effects during relaxation and recovery. The wood flooring on the ground floor is made of untreated local larch strips. On the inside, the wood-frame wall cavities are filled with vapor-permeable blown-in cellulose insulation and finished with birch plywood panels—which are invisibly fastened to the counter battens along the tongue-and-groove joints—to form a contrast with the dark, aged wood of the existing structure. This choice of materials also highlights the difference between old and new on the inside. A vapor-permeable layer of windproof building paper provides resistance to wind. The inserted ceiling made of solid wood and the birch plywood paneling on its underside complement the design concept. Again, all of these wood surfaces are left untreated so that the open pores can play their part in enhancing a healthy indoor climate.

The large-scale glazing across the facade of the new building is recessed to avoid overheating from the sun during summer. The wood-framed windows come from the region and have a good environmental performance. The entire roof is refinished with hand-split larch shingles from the region, insulated with cellulose, and waterproofed with a loosely installed flexible polyolefin (FPO) membrane. Since the membrane contains no plasticizers and was installed loosely, it will be easy to recycle this material later. On the inside, cement-bonded particleboards are used as a vapor retarder and for fire protection. The strategy of leaving surface areas untreated and avoiding indoor air pollutants was also pushed through in the bathroom area by in-

stalling wood paneling there as well; only the walls surrounding the bathtub were finished with mosaic tiles on cement backer boards.

For individual use, a fireplace is integrated into the living space. When relaxing in the adjacent seats, the radiant heat can be absorbed directly. The basic heating demand of the building is provided by a heat pump that operates with a downhole heat exchanger. Setting an example, the electricity is supplied by a local provider and is generated 100% by renewable hydropower. The heat is distributed through radiators that are integrated into the wall construction; as a result, the wood surface areas emit radiant heat. The ventilation is low-tech and thus manual; the spatial structure connecting the various floors is ideally suited for cross ventilation.

The new spatial design of the house
creates a sequence of
different consecutive living spaces.

Project	Casa C
Architect	Camponovo Baumgartner Architekten CBA
Client	Private
Location	Reckingen, Switzerland
Completion	2012
Gross floor area	209 m², usable area 114 m²
Construction cost	600,000 CHF
Efficiency standard / certification	Insulation meets Minergie Standard
Annual heating energy demand	96.04 kWh/m²a
Annual primary energy demand	Information not available
U-value exterior wall	0.18 W/m²K
U-value roof	0.138 W/m²K

Sources   cb-arch.ch
           proholz.at/architektur/detail/casa-c/
           Archdaily.com/492624/casa-c-camponovo-baumgartner-architekten, CBA, Presentation Casa C

Ground floor

First upper floor

Second upper floor

Floor plan, scale 1:250

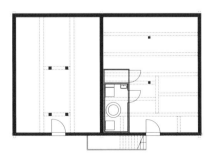

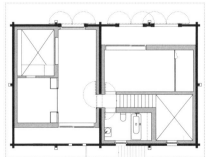

Residential Buildings

The challenging site with its slope and longish layout
resulted in a long stretched building form
with a pitched roof that follows local tradition and
accommodates all functions under one roof.

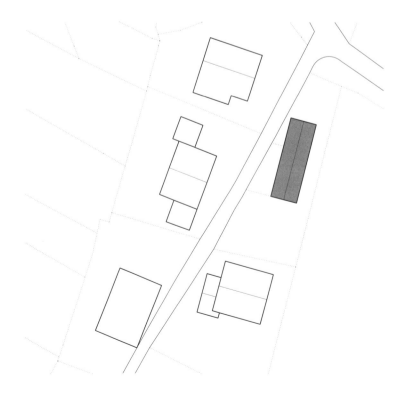

Site plan, scale 1:1000

House for Julia and Björn
Egg, Austria

The house for Julia and Björn, located in the village neighborhood of Egg in the Vorarlberg region of Austria, is rooted in the rural traditions of the region, which found contemporary interpretation through the consistent use of modern wood construction techniques. In cooperation with the architectural office of Innauer Matt Architekten, the clients, who work in the creative field of fashion and graphic design, created a home that is both simple and refined. The challenging site with its slope and longish layout resulted in a long stretched building form with a pitched roof that follows local tradition and accommodates all functions under one roof. As a result, the garage is integrated as are the outdoor seating areas and the utility rooms facing the slope. This leads to a zoning of the rooms that follows the recommendations of building biology exactly: to the north and to the road on the ground floor, ancillary rooms and staircase; on the floor facing the slope, access, pantry, basement, and utility rooms; and to the south across two floors, living and bedrooms with views.

The building concept is rounded off with the recessed shaded patios: one of them is located to the west below the garage to avoid toxic fumes reaching the living spaces (also to provide sufficient distance from exposure to automobile source), and the other one is located to the east on the same side as the kitchen, facing the morning sun. The chosen form of the building is consistent with the rural setting, but

the large-scale glazing of the entrance, which provides a direct view into the generous as well as comfortable design of the interior, exudes an air of urbanity with a close connection to nature. The entrance is like a glass showcase that attracts attention and welcomes visitors.

In line with the chalet style of rural building traditions, the access floor above the lower ground floor is completed as a highly insulated heavy timber structure, but otherwise prefabricated elements are used and the roof overhangs are small, following modern building practices. The lower ground floor, which is partly built into the slope and offers direct access to the garden, was constructed with waterproof concrete over a layer of extruded polystyrene insulation where in contact with the ground. Foam glass insulation would be a good alternative here.

The wood wool used for the insulation of the roof and exterior walls is consistent with building biology recommendations because this material supports vapor diffusion and moisture transfer via capillary action with the additional benefit of good environmental performance. Exterior wall assemblies open to diffusion are recommended because they allow moisture that has infiltrated into such a wall to find its way out again easily. With this in mind, the building envelope of the house for Julia and Björn contains a vapor-permeable wind barrier on the outside, which is also necessary due to the open nature of the siding.

Spruce from the client's own forest was used for the roughly sawn and soaped wood flooring as well as for built-in furnishings, staircase, and wall cabinets.

Project	House for Julia and Björn
Architect	Innauer Matt Architekten
Client	Private
Location	Egg, Austria
Completion	2013
Gross floor area	230 m², usable area 191 m²
Construction cost	500,000 EUR
Efficiency standard / certification	Information not available
Annual heating energy demand	20 kWh/m²a
Annual primary energy demand	14 kWh/m²a
U-value exterior wall	0.11 W/m²K
U-value roof	0.11 W/m²K
Awards	Haus des Jahres 2015 [Home of the Year], Best Architects Award 2015
	Holzbaupreis Vorarlberg 2015 [Wood Building Award Voralberg]

Sources   innauer-matt.com
           Martha Miklin, Die Hinterfrager, faq-bregenzerwald.com
           For Julia and Björn, baunetz.de, 12 February.2015
           Archdaily.com/597258/haus-fur-julia-und-bjorn-innauer-matt-architekten

The wood for the frames and jambs of the custom-crafted windows also comes from the local forest. The white oil finish protects the windows from the weather and gives the otherwise simple facade a refined touch. The slats of the untreated wood siding will turn gray over time and can be replaced without much effort as needed. This provides a good structural preservation of the wood, and any weathered wood can be replaced and used for heating the house by burning it in the wood boiler.

And again, the wood for the floor, wall, ceiling, and furnishing surfaces comes from the client's own forest, which has a positive effect on the carbon footprint of the building, since locally harvested timber requires only short transport routes, supports the local economy, and employs local workers. Spruce from the client's own forest was used for the roughly sawn and soaped wood flooring as well as for built-in furnishings, staircase, and wall closets. The silver fir harvested by the clients was also used roughly sawn and untreated, covering the sloped ceiling and partition walls in the bedrooms on the upper floors. The open-pore structure of the untreated wood surfaces has a positive impact on indoor climate. Humidity can be buffered and released as needed. With a depth of only 20 to 30 mm, vapor-permeable and hygroscopic interior surfaces can have a positive effect on indoor climate. The surface temperature of the wood surfaces remains warm to the touch due to the heat storage capacity of the wood. The plaster was mixed on-site with marble dust. It was then manually applied to the surfaces of the reinforced concrete walls, ceilings, and the firebricks around the boiler on the lower ground level, offering a soothing contrast to the wood furnishings. The haptic properties of the surfaces are a feast for the eyes and a joy to touch.

The building technology in the house for Julia and Björn is kept simple as well. The required heating energy is generated by the log-burning boiler on the lower ground level, which has a comfortable bench integrated in the living space. The wood-burning boiler supplies energy for both the heating and the domestic hot water. The boiler itself and the heating elements embedded in the reinforced concrete walls not only heat the house, but also accelerate the reduction of moisture in the new construction. The floor heating surfaces in the entrance areas and bathrooms on the upper floors are also powered by the wood-burning boiler.

A solar thermal system mounted on the roof adds to the heat supply so that the domestic hot water can be heated by a renewable energy source in summer. Ventilation is simple and efficient: the built-in intake and exhaust air ventilation system with heat recovery supplies fresh air to the living spaces and bedrooms, while extracting used air from the dining and entrance areas.

Apart from providing weather protection, the spaced fir slats also allow the inner layers of the building to shine through, making it possible to integrate a large bathroom window and sun shades for the patio to the west as semipermeable elements.

Ground floor

First upper floor

Second upper floor

Floor plan, scale 1:400

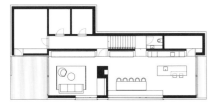

The single-level farmyard house designed by Kühnlein
Architektur has an H-shaped floor plan that
creates an intimate inner courtyard surrounded by the
same siding material and that combines the
two archetypal wings to form a monolithic ensemble.

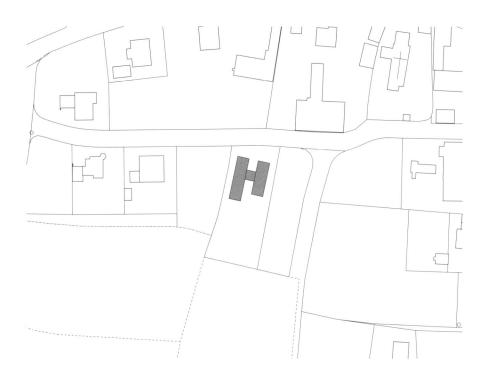

Site plan, scale 1:2000

The House of Wood
Neumarkt, Upper Palatinate, Germany

In the transition zone between the village of Neumarkt in the Upper Palatinate and its surrounding landscape, a residence was built in 2014 that stands out with its simple lines and its dedication to sustainability. The single-level farmyard house designed by Kühnlein Architektur has an H-shaped floor plan with an inviting entrance area and an intimate inner courtyard. The boundary of the private courtyard following the exterior wall combines the two archetypal wings to form a monolithic ensemble and highlights the homogeneity of the chosen material and the simplicity of the design. The wood slats used across the openings to the outside underscore the sculpted effect, giving the facade a poetic, shimmering appearance. The reduced design language of the building incorporates village roots and the human scale, translating them into contemporary architecture. The interior is clearly structured and well zoned in building biology terms. The bedrooms are located to the southeast and the kitchen and living spaces to the southwest. Furthermore, the floor plan with the connecting entrance building opens to the inner courtyard at the back as well as to the landscape facing southwest. In this natural setting, the untreated larch slat siding of the exterior wall will weather into a silver-gray patina over time and ultimately blend into the surrounding landscape. Only the oiled larch window frames will then provide a contrast.

The interior design also relies on the simplicity of healthy building materials. To that end, the architect Michael Kühnlein Jr explains: "If you have such an amazing building material, there is no need to hide it. Rather it should be visible. This follows the old tradition of building with wood in which a wood structure would not be concealed either."[1] The building was completed as a load-bearing mass timber construction. The five-layer cross-laminated timber panels show off the visual quality of pure wood in the interior. Without any additional surface treatment, the environmental performance of this building material is perfect. The solid wood panels can also be easily reused at the end of their life cycle. The interior furnishings are a reflection of the predominant material, so the scrap wood from the solid wall panels was used, for example, to fashion tables. This was the first step of upcycling building material. Regarding the structural integrity of the building, mass timber construction has the advantage of making it possible to use large-scale systems of folded plates. Stiffened by diagonal sheathing of roughly sawn wood, the archetypal appeal also carries over to the interior spaces. Since the form of the pitched roof is visible from the inside, a generous, light-flooded space is created. Each of the two children's bedrooms features a loft above the small bathroom and the utility room, reaching up to the ridge of the roof. Aside from wood, another material that dominates the interior design is copper, which was used in fixtures, lighting elements, and the switch system with its exposed copper pipes that contain the wiring. This is an example of how diligently the formal design concept was followed.

With regard to other building materials, the architects chose materials that satisfy the requirements of building biology. The exterior wall

and the roofs benefit from wood fiber insulation because the thermal capacity of the insulation material also ensures effective protection against overheating in summer. On the inside, a system of sheer curtains across the generous glazing facing the patio supports a well-balanced room temperature by reducing the penetration of sunlight during summer, while keeping the heat inside the house during winter. The glazing of the connecting structure is also shielded from solar overexposure with larch wood slats. In addition, the green roof acts as a thermal buffer. The overall thermal insulation of the building is so good that the geothermal heat pump along with the fireplace only need to be used for a few days in winter. In addition to the vapor-permeable wood surfaces, the radiant heat released across the solid oak flooring contributes to a great indoor climate. Due to their good thermal storage capacity, wood floors are always warm to the touch.

To increase the capacity of storing solar gains or to retain the heat longer indoors, masonry walls with a higher thermal diffusivity such as walls made of rammed earth or sand-lime bricks can serve as a reasonable alternative according to building biology. The partition walls in this project were made of a single material just like the structural mass timber panels: solid wood. To be able to individually control the heat in the bathrooms as needed, wall heating units were mounted behind water-resistant wood fiberboards.

It was a conscious choice to use as little building technology as possible. The geothermal heat pump is the source of renewable energy for heating and domestic hot water. Electricity is provided by a solar power system installed on a separate tool shed. This is also where the inverter, which emits magnetic fields, is located, that is, far away from living spaces. For the lighting system, flicker-reduced warm white LED lamps were chosen, as well as incandescent lamps whose light color corresponds to natural daylight at dusk and whose color rendering properties are particularly good. Though standard incandescent lamps have not been available since 2012, the designer incandescent lamps used here have the advantage of being flicker-free and therefore are especially well suited for healthy lighting conditions. Incandescent lamps consume quite a large amount of electricity when compared with other light sources. However, the exceptional light quality and the use of renewable electricity make their use acceptable in this case. Furthermore, the electrical wiring design follows a star-like pattern and allows the lamps to be adjusted individually, thereby ensuring low EMF exposure levels.

The ventilation of the building is provided by manual window ventilation, which keeps the technology requirements to a minimum. To reduce water consumption, a rainwater tank collects rainwater for the irrigation of the green areas.

The archetypal appeal also carries over to the interior
spaces. Since the form of the pitched roof is
visible from the inside, a generous, light-flooded
space is created.

Project	The House of Wood
Architect	Kühnlein Architektur
Client	Private
Location	Neumarkt, Upper Palatinate, Germany
Completion	October 2014
Gross floor area	Usable area 210 m²
Construction cost	500,000 EUR
Efficiency standard / certification	KfW Energy Efficiency House 55
Annual heating energy demand	47.61 kWh/m²a
Annual primary energy demand	43.36 kWh/m²a
U-value exterior wall	0.16 W/m²K
U-value roof	0.13 W/m²K

Endnote   1 zmh.com/hausbau/beispiele-hausbau/portrait/haus-kuehnlein.html (accessed on 19 March 2017).
Sources   kuehnlein-architektur.de
             Wladimir Kaminer and Wolfgang Bachmann, Häuser des Jahres 2015, Munich: Callwey Verlag 2015
             Die-besten-einfamilienhaeuser.de/holzhaus-mit-hof/

In this natural setting, the untreated larch slat siding of the exterior wall will weather into a silver-gray patina over time and ultimately blend into the surrounding landscape.

Floor plan, scale 1:250

Maison Marly
Marly-le-Roi, France

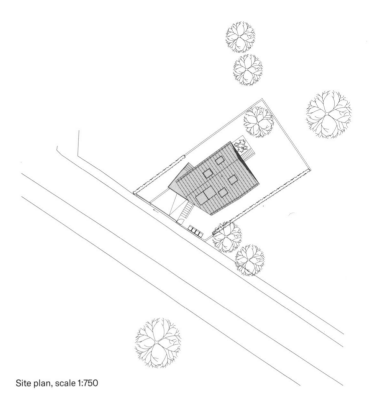

Site plan, scale 1:750

The expressive design of the single-family house in Marly-le-Roi, a small town 15 km west of Paris, stands out in the rather secluded and quiet neighborhood, which is otherwise defined by many hedges. The new Maison Marly by Karawitz Architecture is a case of surprisingly modern and urban understatement. It is not only the shimmering appearance of the building caused by the semipermeable siding, but also the monolithic, crystalline form that reveals the self-assurance and maturity of the residence, completed in 2015, to the observer. The elements that decided the design of this house were the building code regulations in terms of spacing and openings, on the one hand, and the homeowner's desire for an urban home, on the other hand. The building has an almost sculpted appeal as it rests on the site. To address the wish for hospitality, the entrance area was lowered to create a generously sheltered front courtyard that welcomes visitors to the home. This space serves as a carport and a protected storage area for firewood, as well as an access to the garden. Since in this process the guest level has been raised from the ground, the structure appears to almost hover in place, playing with the perceptions of "weight" and "lightness." The openings in the uniform and angular facade were decided based on their use. All openings—large openings facing the patio to the south, deliberate openings from the living spaces into the garden, and openings in the bedrooms pointing to the sky—not only meet functional requirements, but they also stage views looking into and out of the house, while at the same time creating a sense of comfort and visually striking moments.

The architects designed the new building true to their firm's philosophy that aims to combine architectural aesthetics with sustainability, building ecology, and energy efficiency, using building methods of passive house and mass timber construction. Only the subterranean level, used temporarily by guests and otherwise intended as a mechanical room, was completed using reinforced concrete with conventional insulation. All other levels were completed as mass timber construction made of glue-laminated timber panels and insulated exclusively with ecologically certified renewable materials, wood fiber insulation boards, and cellulose. This optimum level of insulation and airtightness reduced the heating energy requirements to such an extent that the central fireplace on the ground level suffices to heat the entire building in winter.

The green building community in France considers Karawitz Architecture at the forefront of energy efficiency, which is why many of the construction tasks are completed with conventional standard solutions. Even in ecological and sustainable projects, their solutions are mainly adjusted to the availability of what the market has to offer, so building materials that come from other regions of Europe may also be used. For the mass timber construction of this building, PEFC- and FSC-certified raw materials were used; however, the cross-laminated timber panels were glued with polyurethane adhesive. In building biology, cross-laminated timber with wood dowels or wood screws rather than adhesives is recommended.

The architects designed the new building using building methods of passive house and mass timber construction. The central fireplace on the ground level suffices to heat the entire building in winter.

Project	Maison Marly
Architect	Karawitz Architecture
Client	Private
Location	Marly-le-Roi, France
Completion	September 2015
Gross floor area	Usable area 145 m²
Construction cost	Information not available
Efficiency standard / certification	Passive house
Annual heating energy demand	20 kWh/m²a
Annual primary energy demand	56.7 kWh/m²a (as calculated based on French regulations)
U-value exterior wall	0.14 W/m²K (mass timber construction), 0.17 W/m²K (reinforced concrete)
U-value roof	0.08 W/m²K

Sources   karawitz.com
Karawitz, press dossier Maison Marly
Rudy Köhler, "Isocyanate und Polyurethane – Fluch oder Segen?," Wohnung + Gesundheit, 151, 2, 2014

Since the visible surfaces are all made from the
same material, the monolithic character of the house
with its almost sculpture-like appearance thus
also continues in the interior. The natural stain the wood
surfaces are finished with preserves the material's
true identity and maintains the vapor permeability and,
by extension, the positive impact on indoor climate.

Since the visible surfaces are all made from the same material, the monolithic character of the house with its almost sculpture-like appearance thus also continues in the interior. The natural stain the wood surfaces are finished with preserves the material's true identity and maintains the vapor permeability and, by extension, the positive impact on indoor climate.

Other than that, wood strips can also be pressure bonded by means of nontoxic adhesives (e.g. natural resin glue, white glue, casein glue). The use of isocyanate-based adhesives (PU or PUR) is less favored in building biology. During the use of the products that contain polyurethane adhesives, no health risks are known; however, the production and processing of these adhesives is associated with ecological and toxicological risks.

Since the visible surfaces are all made from the same material in this mass timber structure, the monolithic character of the house with its almost sculpture-like appearance thus also continues in the interior. A natural stain gives all wood surfaces a pleasantly light hue, preserves the true identity of the material, and maintains the high vapor permeability and, by extension, the positive impact on indoor climate. The floating floor screed made it possible to give the family the sound insulation they needed in the building. The screed was finished and polished, but left exposed with an eye to homogeneity and preserving the true identity of the material. The surface treatments,

as recommended by building biology, include oiling and waxing, as well as clay-casein finishes that produce especially robust high-quality surfaces. Surfaces with natural finishes also prevent a buildup of static electricity and promote a healthy indoor climate.

The larch siding of the Maison Marly is installed over wood fiber insulation boards with a ventilated rainscreen. The graying stain enhances the process of aging and protects the wood against the elements. The triple-glazed wood-aluminum windows complement the highly energy-efficient building envelope. The level of airtightness required by the passive house standard led to the installation of a ventilation system with heat recovery. The house is powered by electricity from a provider that relies on renewable energy sources. Thus the decentralized domestic hot water system, but also the radiators in the guest rooms, can be powered by green power. In a passive house, the decentralized heating of service water is often the more sensible alternative, since a centralized heating system for this water is not necessary for a large part of the year. This allows the hot water piping to be kept to a minimum. The cold water piping can be run to the point of use where the water is heated, thereby contributing to a safer water system.

To address the wish for hospitality, the entrance area was lowered to create a generously sheltered front courtyard that welcomes visitors to the home.

Lower ground floor

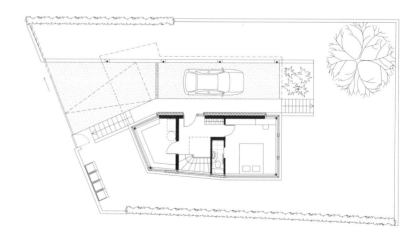

Since in this process the guest level has been raised from the ground, the structure appears to almost hover in place, playing with the perceptions of "weight" and "lightness."

Ground floor

Upper floor

Floor plans, scale 1:250

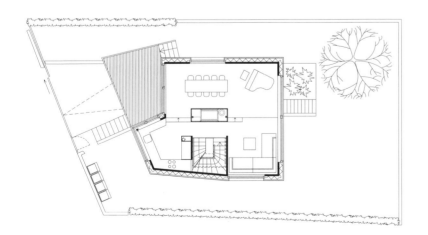

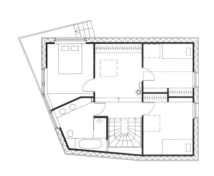

The ecologically minded and aesthetically appealing
design concept of the Haussicht Design House,
a singular structure inspired by shipbuilding as one of
the original forms of wood construction, has been
developed from the inside out—both as a view to
the outside and into the future of housing and living.

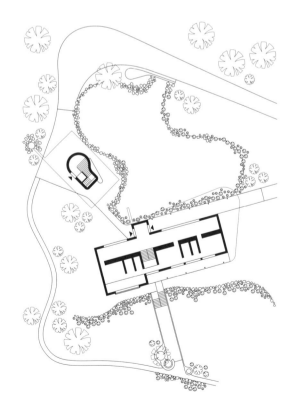

Site plan, scale 1:750

Haussicht Design House
Erkheim, Germany

Based on the motto "Realizing visions—showing it can be done!", it is the intent of the Haussicht project to show new dimensions of doing wood architecture in an ecological and healthy way. This means that ecologically minded and aesthetically appealing wood construction should combine sustainability not only with ecological substance, quality, and enduring value, but also with beauty, enjoyment, and joy of life. The project, which combines all of these elements with precision and poetry, was a collaboration between Baufritz—the green building pioneer in the Allgäu region—and the Swiss designer Alfredo Häberli assisted by the architect Stephan Rehm. It aims to offer a new take on prefabricated housing and puts people at the center of the design. The design concept has been developed from the inside out—both as a view to the outside and into the future of housing and living. The result is a singular structure inspired by shipbuilding—one of the original forms of wood construction—paired with another smaller detached "Stöckli," a barrier-free retirement home.[1]

Wood as a sustainable building material with high-tech qualities is used in many different ways here. The bow-like roof, the nature-inspired organic forms, the quality of the interior furnishings, as well as the structural challenges posed by the generous, unsupported open spaces show the high performance of the selected building material. The ground floor layout is defined by tranquility and openness. A wall extending the length of the building with an integrated, ceiling-high storage cabinet at the bedroom level delineates the north and south zones by serving as a divider, a piece of furniture, and a load-bearing structure. The rooms are aligned as "berths" facing south, while sliding elements allow for flexible floor area variations and space correlations. On the floor with the living spaces, the cooking and dining area is an open space with a three-sided link to the freely formed deck. A flexible, platform-like seating system—the "media berth"—makes the space adaptable for various possible uses. The facade is integrated into the living space, creating a quality space to enjoy, while at the same time maximizing the amount of daylight exposure. Fixed and sliding solar control elements on the exterior reduce the effect of summer heat.

The expressive architecture of the structure was brought to life using system construction: The wood-panel construction uses large elements made of spruce and larch, which were tested for harmful substances. The building is insulated with Baufritz wood chip insulation (HOIZ), which is enhanced with whey and soda and has been awarded numerous certificates. A shielding panel against electromagnetic radiation is just as much part of the exterior wall assembly as is an installation cavity on the interior side. Airtight and windproof layers open to diffusion complete the exterior system wall assembly. The spruce siding extends over the entire height of the building and was finished with an eco-friendly, nontoxic, vapor-permeable alkali silicate-based paint (physical mode of action), which enhances the graying process of the wood. The roof was completed with a layer of ventilated sheet metal.

Despite the generous areas of glazing, the highly insulated building envelope with its triple thermal insulation glazing and the on-demand ventilation system with occupancy and air quality sensors achieves the rating for a KfW Efficiency House 55 awarded by the German-government owned development bank KfW. This was also possible due to the low-temperature floor heating system, which is powered by renewable energies and also offers cooling in summer. The eTank, an underground system to store heat, is also part of this system. Most of the building technology is barely visible: the photovoltaic/thermal (PVT) solar panels are mounted on the mono-pitched roof, the cooling system is integrated into the ceiling, the eTank is buried underground, and the electrical bus system of the intelligent building automation shows only as a design object in the form of a touch panel.

The solar energy stored as heat makes it possible for the innovative heat pump to achieve an exceptional seasonal performance factor of 7 (SPF 7), making it a highly efficient ecological alternative. In addition, the thermally activated photovoltaic modules increase the yield of electricity by reducing the heat buildup. The renewable electricity is stored in batteries and used to feed the mechanical, electrical, and plumbing systems, as well as the in-house electric car charging station. In addition to the shielding panel in the exterior wall, shielded building wiring was used to provide protection against exposure to artificial electromagnetic fields. The steel used for structural support was demagnetized to reduce the distortion of the Earth's magnetic field as much as possible. For lighting, energy-efficient and nearly flicker-free LED systems were chosen.

Building ecology, healthy living, and sustainability were vitally important for selecting the equipment and furnishings of the Haussicht Design House. Wall surfaces were painted with solvent-free mineral paint; the oak of the interiors is oiled. All furniture, lamps, textiles, and accessories were subject to an indoor air quality analysis to ensure their safety. This led to the use of natural latex for the upholstery of the media berth and a triple oiling process for the oak bathtub intended for everyday use. According to Dagmar Fritz-Kramer, the managing director of Baufritz, building materials should be used true to their inherent characteristics and "in as pure a state as possible. Anything you bake together cannot be separated later."[2]

At 300 square meters, the main house of the Haussicht Design House offers a generous amount of space. The approach taken with this project is what is of primary importance to Alfredo Häberli; hence, the size is initially of less importance. For Dagmar Fritz-Kramer, the nature-based approach is paramount, analogous to the cradle-to-cradle principle: "We could live ... in abundance, just from what nature gives us. We only need to succeed at using renewable resources in such a way that we will cause no damage and produce no waste."[3]

Building ecology, healthy living, and sustainability
were vitally important for selecting the
equipment and furnishings of the Haussicht Design
House. This led to a triple oiling process
for the oak bathtub intended for everyday use.

Project	Haussicht
Architect	Baufritz (Stephan Rehm) with Alfredo Häberli
Client	Bau-Fritz GmbH & Co. KG
Location	Erkheim, Germany
Completion	2016
Gross floor area	Usable area 320 m²
Construction cost	4,560 EUR per m² (from top of basement)
Efficiency standard / certification	KfW Energy Efficiency House 55
Annual heating energy demand	22.3 kWh/m²a
Annual primary energy demand	18.56 kWh/m²a
U-value exterior wall	0.20 W/m²K
U-value roof	0.16 W/m²K

Endnotes   1 Press release Haussicht–Visionen vom Wohnen / Baufritz_Haussicht_Booklet_5849.pdf (accessed on 03 March 2017)
             2 Film Baufritz Haussicht–Präzision + Poesie (accessed on 03 March 2017)
             3 Haussicht booklet (as endnote 1), p. 12 (accessed on 03 March 2017)
Sources   baufritz.com/lu/architektur-und-haeuser/designhaus/konzepthaus-haussicht/#site
             Baufritz, Pressrelease Haussicht
             Alfredo-haeberli.com/work/architecture/6-217/haussicht
             Jürgen Brandenburger, "Ökologische Baukultur gepaart mit außergewöhnlichem Design," Inspiration DESIGN! Architektur & Design, 01, 2017
             Film of project: Baufritz Haussicht – Präzision + Poesie / Handwerk + Design, vimeo.com

A wall extending the length of the building with an integrated, ceiling-high storage cabinet at the bedroom level separates the north and south zones by serving as a divider, a piece of furniture, and a load-bearing structure. Sliding elements allow for flexible floor area variations.

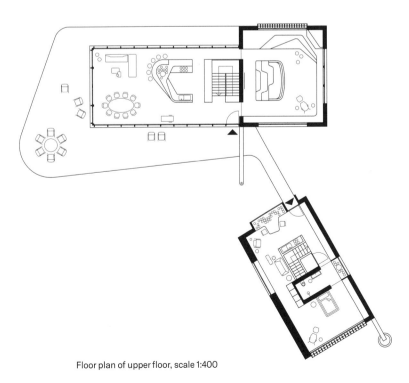

Floor plan of upper floor, scale 1:400

The initiative of "Seven Ecological Projects for Amsterdam" by two architects—who are also trained as building biology consultants and building historians—was the starting point for developing a sustainable and healthy method to restore old buildings in Amsterdam.

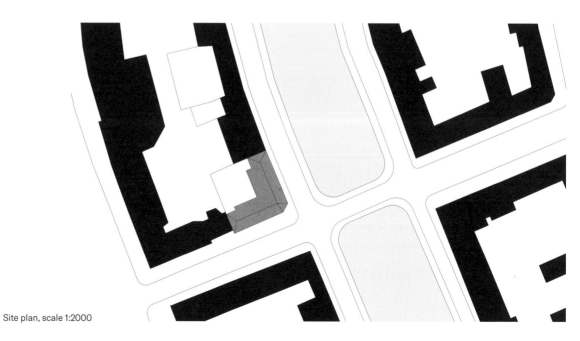

Site plan, scale 1:2000

De Potgieter School
Amsterdam, The Netherlands

The impact of the Potgieter School in Amsterdam has a special history. The initiative of "Seven Ecological Projects for Amsterdam" by two architects—who also trained as building biology consultants and building historians—was the starting point for developing a sustainable and healthy method to restore old buildings in Amsterdam, a city with more than 7,000 historic buildings. The work of Daniel Höwekamp and Luigi Pucciano—the founders of the architectural firm aayu architects—on this project in the historic Oud-West neighborhood led the Historic Preservation and Archeology Office to recommend their type of restoration as a model for the revitalization of historic buildings, and the Climate and Energy Department of the municipality to consider this method as a step into a sustainable future. Even though awareness of building biology is growing only slowly in the Netherlands, certain topics such as healthy living spaces and healthy indoor air quality have gained in popularity. At the same time, energy saving potentials, and by extension cost savings, are important when building in a sustainable and ecological manner. The architects therefore made it their mission to focus on both the building biology and energy efficiency aspects in this model restoration project. In 2010, the architects were asked to create a cost-neutral design for the restoration of the historic primary school building from 1886, which would convert the school building into an energy-efficient, building biology-based neighborhood center including a daycare facility for children.

The energy concept was ambitious, also taking building science aspects into account: Mounted on the roof and invisible from the canal, the gas/air-source heat pump and the solar power system supply renewable energy. The CO_2-controlled mechanical ventilation system operates with a heat recovery system, while a low-temperature heating system with active floor and wall zones provides thermal comfort through radiant heat. The roof and the ground level floor have a 300 mm thick layer of cellulose insulation installed, and the exterior wall features a 60 mm thick interior wood fiber insulation over a base coat of clay plaster. The windows of the historic building received an energy upgrade too. By increasing the depth of the window frames by 20 mm on the inside, it became possible to use insulated glazing with solid oak sash bars and glass spacers. As a result, the historical appearance of the glazing and the option of manual window ventilation could be preserved. The daylight-controlled LED lighting system also plays its part in saving energy. The above-described energy-saving measures allowed the architects to preserve the historic appearance and value of the building as a landmark and thus ensured the future viability of this historic building.

Further building biology measures create a healthy indoor climate and promote a holistic use of the building. In line with finishes used historically to promote humidity regulation, a clay plaster was chosen for the interior. Since the clay plaster and the wood fiber insulation are both open to diffusion, a high vapor permeability can be maintained. The clay plaster also absorbs harmful air pollutants and in combination with the radiant heating system contributes to exceptional indoor air quality.

To save resources and to avoid construction waste, all decisions regarding the building materials and methods were based on their durability, adaptability, disassembly, and recyclability following the cradle-to-cradle principles. The design was developed taking all these factors into account, resulting in beautiful details, for example, glazed doors in the entrance hall incorporating distressed steel profiles aged with vinegar and oil to give them a rusted appearance, or the solid wood components like the oiled oak doors leading to the seminar and common rooms.

The rooms were returned to their original dimensions after the removal of the suspended ceilings, which had been added in the 1970s. This made it possible to reuse materials, turning the building into its own raw material depot during the restoration. The dismantled wood components were used to create kitchen cabinets and a garden shed in the courtyard. Worn-down wooden stairs were refinished, flipped, and used again "just like in Roman times," as the architects like to say. The acoustics of the existing rooms with their restored high ceilings are regulated with a sound-absorbing gypsum ceiling.

The mechanical, electrical, and plumbing systems were also chosen to meet the requirements of building biology, low maintenance, and sustainability. As a result, the ductwork of the ventilation system is not visible, yet still accessible. The building wiring follows a star-like pattern with dedicated circuits to each room to minimize the spread of ELF magnetic fields. Rainwater is collected in a 20,000-liter rainwater bag in the crawlspace, which is then used to flush the toilets. For hygiene and children's health reasons, stainless steel piping was chosen for the drinking water pipes. The crawlspace was also refurbished during the project by adding a layer of shells as a capillary break that helps regulate the humidity at this lower level.

And the green areas also demonstrate the project's commitment to an integrated design concept. The green roof with its rooftop garden enhances urban biodiversity. The mass of this surface area acts as a summer heat shield (heat absorber) for the kindergarten sleeping area underneath. The water-buffering capacity of the green roof also makes it possible to use water sustainably. In addition, "suspended" vegetable gardens in the courtyard of the complex serve as edible gardens for the children and raise awareness about the origin and cultivation of food. Furthermore, a bamboo garden invites the children to explore nature and provides private spaces to retreat to.

The building was restored with the needs of children and the environment in mind. With regard to health, children require more protection than adults. In particular, the health of small children and, indeed, the ecosystem as a whole should be protected. A biological or architectural monument shows—in the words of the architects— its past, the present builds upon this past, offering optimal comfort and health, and then there will only be "great things in store" for the occupants in the future.[1]

The rooms were returned to their original dimensions
after the removal of the suspended ceilings,
which had been added in the 1970s. This made it possible
to reuse materials. The dismantled wood components were used to create kitchen cabinets and a garden
shed in the courtyard.

Project	De Potgieter School
Architect	aayu architects, Daniel Höwekamp, Luigi Pucciano
Client	City of Amsterdam, Amsterdam Stadsdeel West
Location	Amsterdam Oud-West, The Netherlands
Completion	2012
Gross floor area	300 m², usable are 250 m²
Construction cost	2,200,000 EUR
Efficiency standard / certification	EPC 0.8 (Energy Performance Certificate)
Annual heating energy demand	Information not available
Annual primary energy demand	Information not available
U-value exterior wall	Information not available
U-value roof	Information not available

Endnote   1 Daniel Höwekamp, "Da Vinci Schule in Amsterdam," Wohnung + Gesundheit, 147, 2, 2013
Sources   www.aayu.eu/en/nieuws/publicaties
            Aayu architecten, Biologisch Monument DE POTGIETER, 2013
            Daniel Höwekamp, "Da Vinci Schule in Amsterdam," Wohnung + Gesundheit, 147, 2, 2013

The green areas also demonstrate the project's commitment to an integrated design concept. Among other things, a bamboo garden invites the children to explore nature and provides private spaces to retreat to.

Floor plan ground floor, scale 1:400

The school was given a new face with the construction
of a two-level pavilion for the fire station
of the volunteer fire department and the extension
of the school.

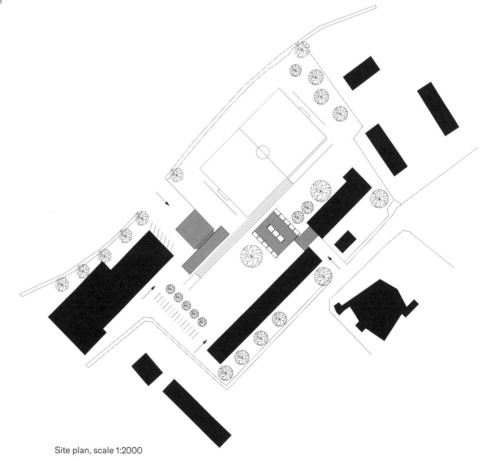

Site plan, scale 1:2000

The Friedensschule School and
Fire Department Annex
Schwäbisch Gmünd, Germany

The Friedensschule in Schwäbisch Gmünd, an interdenominational school, has been offering primary and lower secondary education in two existing buildings since the 1950s. The demolition of a run-down wing gave the municipality the opportunity to expand the school and build a much-needed fire station. The freelance architect and building biology professional Christoph Bijok developed a concept to restore the urban development area at the beginning of the 2000s. The school was given a new face with the construction of a two-level pavilion for the fire station of the volunteer fire department and the extension of the school. A new entrance portal was added, as was a new structure connecting the two wings of the school, which accommodates special service areas and whose exterior spaces are also accessible to the public. The existing trees here were left standing, and the excavation material and uncontaminated demolition material were reused in the landscaping of this area. The fire station with its social wing creates a protective "back" to the south. It is visually linked to the school structure by the use of the same material. The pavilion connects both school wings via the glazed, unheated entrance portal, gives structure to the recess areas, and frames the new space on the eastern end.

The ground level of the pavilion is used for multiple functions, for example, as a full-day care facility including a kitchen and as a music room. The movable wall elements also make it possible to use this level as an event hall for musical performances and municipal meetings. The upper level of the pavilion accommodates the teachers' area, which can

also be used by the students because the administrative office, student library, and "quiet study areas" designed as unheated atria set in front of the glass facades are also located there. These glass facades facing west/east define the open appearance of the building, which otherwise is built as a heavy timber structure closed to the south and north. The atria, which serve as buffer zones for indoor climate, create a temperate zone that reduces temperature fluctuations in the interior rooms. In winter, this helps to limit cold air surges, unpleasant air circulation, and radiation cooling. Furthermore, the penetration of summer heat is regulated with blinds. On the ground floor, the indoor climate is also supported by structural measures. This level is completely glazed and therefore recessed along its entire length. In summer, the upper level and the deciduous trees around the building provide ample shade, and in winter they expose the ground floor to the warmth from the sun. The connecting, unheated entrance structure also gives the building a temperate buffer space that captures solar heat during cold weather. In addition, the extensively planted green roof both insulates and protects the building below.

The heavy timber construction of the exterior walls was fitted with vapor-permeable solid wood panels and insulated with blown-in cellulose. On the outside, the larch siding with its ventilated rainscreen is protected with an oil finish. The frame of the structure was stiffened vertically with diagonal steel rods mounted on the exterior of the atria to resist tensile and compressive forces. The distance established between the

The pavilion connects both school wings via the glazed, unheated entrance portal. In winter, this entrance structure also serves as a temperate buffer zone that captures solar heat.

steel elements and the users ensures that the steel's distortion of the Earth's magnetic field does not affect the users in the indoor spaces. The horizontal stiffness of the structure is achieved by the wooden box ceiling, which functions as a slab here. The interior sides of this ceiling and the exterior walls are made of cross-laminated spruce panels (three layers) whose wood is left exposed and finished with colorless wax. The parquet floors are also treated with a colorless wax finish that is vapor-permeable and nontoxic, contributing to a healthy electro- and indoor climate.

The noise control required in school buildings is provided through structural and acoustic means. A layer of sound-absorbing aggregate is inserted as additional mass in the wooden box ceiling. The rooms requiring confidentiality on the teacher's level were completed as sound transmission loss barrier walls whose wood-frame walls are acoustically uncoupled and insulated with cellulose. Aside from the required airborne sound insulation inside the wooden box ceiling, cellulose fibers and a floating industrial parquet were installed for structure-borne sound insulation. The wood ceilings also feature sound-absorbing finishes. To comply with the German F30 B fire protection requirements for stiffening elements, the thickness of the uppermost wood layer of the ceiling system was increased to 40 mm to be thicker than the standard specifications. The elements of the load-bearing structure made of laminated timber were also calculated to meet the fire protection requirements. The ceiling construction houses components of the ventilation system.

Since the ceiling assembly is made of glued-laminated spruce certified to be nontoxic, it was possible to use wood channels for the ventilation system, without any additional lining or ductwork. For the ventilation system of the extension, an energy-efficient cross-flow heat exchanger was installed that can also be used for cooling in summer as needed. The intake air is preconditioned via an earth tube both in summer and winter. The heating requirements of the new structures—including both the school extension and the fire station—are covered by the existing gas heating system, which was modernized during the renovation of the existing buildings.

Some of the original design ideas had to be abandoned, such as the wood pellet heating system, the wall heating system in the pavilion, and the photovoltaic system on the roof of the fire station. One of the reasons being that it was not possible to establish how the operational savings would offset the expense of the investment in this publicly funded project. That way the building could be built within the cost constraints, while implementing building methods based on building biology, resource efficiency, and ecology. An important aspect of the ecologically enhanced building is the positive influence of the material wood on mood. Besides the school's current, more artistic approach to education with regular music and theater activities, it also helps take the edge off the potential for aggression.

The noise control required in school buildings is provided through structural and acoustic means. A layer of sound-absorbing aggregate is inserted as additional mass in the wooden box ceiling. The wood ceilings also feature sound-absorbing finishes.

Project	The Friedensschule School and Fire Department Annex
Architect	Christoph Bijok
Client	The City of Schwäbisch Gmünd
Location	Schwäbisch Gmünd, Germany
Completion	2007
Gross floor area	Usable area: school 678 m² / fire department annex 517 m²
Construction cost	School 1,688,000 EUR / fire department 865,000 EUR
Efficiency standard / certification	Low-energy house meets EnEV 2001
Annual heating energy demand	55 kWh/m²a
Annual primary energy demand	Information not available
U-value exterior wall	0.25 W/m²K
U-value roof	0.21 W/m²K
Awards	Deutscher Holzbaupreis 2007, Anerkennung
	[German Wood Construction Award, Honorary Mention]

Sources   christophbijok.de
Christoph Bijok, Feuerwehrhaus und Erweiterung der Friedensschule in Schwäbisch Gmünd, zum 12. Internationalen Holzbauforum 2006
[Fire Department Building and the Friedensschule School Annex in Schwäbisch Gmünd,
12th International Holzbauforum Construction Conference, 2006]

The fire station with its social wing creates a protective "back" to the north of the exterior spaces that are also accessible to the public. In this area, the existing trees were left standing, and the excavation material and uncontaminated demolition material were reused in the landscaping.

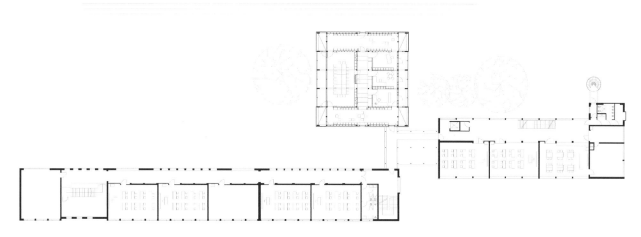

Floor plan upper floor, scale 1:750

To bring the world of plants closer to the public, especially to the younger generations, Gale & Snowden Architects built the Peter Buckley Learning Centre of the Royal Horticultural Society in the gardens of Rosemoor following the principles of building biology.

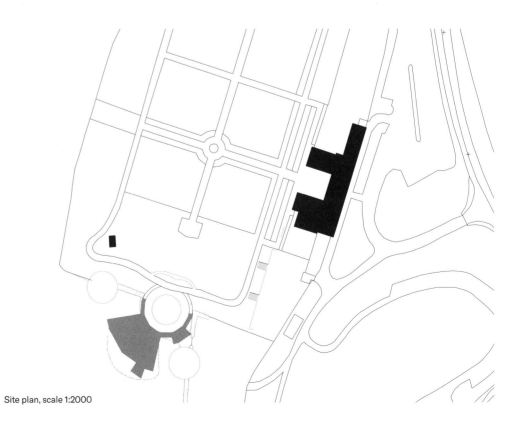

Site plan, scale 1:2000

RHS Peter Buckley Learning Centre
Rosemoor, Devon, England

The more than 200-year-old Royal Horticultural Society (RHS) is dedicated to the advancement and improvement of the science, art, and practice of horticulture. It is the vision of the RHS to enrich everyone's life through plants. This British organization with four large garden areas spread over the United Kingdom supports such principles as improving human health, building stronger communities, improving food security, reducing waste, building resilience, fostering education in the next generation, and protecting plant health. To bring the world of plants closer to the public, especially to the younger generations, Gale & Snowden Architects built the Peter Buckley Learning Centre in the gardens of Rosemoor, nestled in a valley in Devon in the southwest of England, following the principles of building biology. Tomas Gartner, a partner at Gale & Snowden and a Building Biology Consultant IBN, is also the cofounder of the Building Biology Association,[1] the British center for building biology. Together with Gale & Snowden, he runs the first Building Biology Consulting Office IBN in the United Kingdom. The center offers consulting services in the field of building biology and, in cooperation with the Institute of Building Biology + Sustainability IBN, provides training for becoming a building biology consultant.

The RHS Rosemoor Garden covers an area of 65 hectares, including 40 hectares of landscaped gardens and 25 hectares of woodlands. The breathtaking and diverse collection of plants is designed to help teach children about nature and gardening through a large variety of age-appropriate courses and seminars. It is meant to encourage and arouse the children's curiosity for flora and fauna. The new building in Rosemoor provides classrooms, a sheltered area for working outside next to the learning garden facing south, as well as other secondary rooms.

The dynamic shape of the building follows the existing axes of the gardens, integrating the learning center into the surrounding landscape. Local craftspeople built the wood-frame structure using sustainably harvested wood from local forests. All wood surfaces, whether larch or red cedar siding or solid oak paneling, are left untreated and exposed to the elements.

Based on simulations for thermal performance and daylighting, technical specifications were defined at an early conceptual stage to optimize the design for the climate conditions specific to the site. As a result, the structure was insulated using cellulose insulation: vapor-permeable and hygroscopic. Since courses are held during the day only, the design simulations focused on the optimal use of daylight, the reduction of overheating in summer, and the increase of passive solar gains. The additional choice of triple glazing and an airtight building envelope resulted in an energy-efficient building whose remaining heating requirements in winter can be covered with a log-burning boiler in combination with a solar thermal system. The use of renewable energies for the heating system in the form of wood from the learning

center's own woodlands gives the building added resilience in line with the principles of the organization. Rainwater harvesting via the large roof areas to irrigate the gardens is also part of this design concept.

The principles of building biology were also applied on the inside to create a healthy indoor climate. Consequently, mineral- and plant-based finishing materials were used, as well as untreated wood surfaces and natural, easy-to-clean linoleum. The natural simplicity of the materials is intentional; a conscious decision was made to avoid building materials containing PVC. For a natural radiant heating system, cross-linked polyethylene (PEX) piping was embedded in the flooring. This type of piping can be readily used in building biology because it is safe to produce (no plasticizers and not contaminating groundwater) and easy to reuse. When used for drinking water piping, temperatures up to 95 °C must be considered. It should be possible to flush the pipes with hot water (70 °C) to prevent the buildup of bacterial film or Legionella bacteria. Since this is a public building, the decision was made to use PEX piping for the drinking water pipes.

Given the intention of the project to create simple operating procedures, the building has an easy-to-use, natural ventilation system that requires little maintenance. The openable windows allow for natural cross ventilation and ensure an optimum fresh air supply. Artificial lighting is provided by an energy-efficient LED lighting system. To use a log-burning boiler, a biomass fuel strategy was conceived. According to this strategy, the trees are harvested two years in advance and classified as firewood a year later, before being split into logs to dry during storage. The wood-burning boiler was also designed to burn the available species of wood as efficiently as possible.

The wood-frame structure is built using sustainably
harvested wood from local forests; the
wood siding is left untreated and exposed
to the elements.

Project	RHS Peter Buckley Learning Centre
Architect	Gale & Snowden Architects
Client	Royal Horticultural Society (RHS)
Location	Rosemoor, Devon, United Kingdom
Completion	2011
Gross floor area	400 m²
Construction cost	1,000,000 GBP
Efficiency standard / certification	Information not available
Annual heating energy demand	Information not available
Annual primary energy demand	Information not available
U-value exterior wall	0.13 W/m²K
U-value roof	0.12 W/m²K

Endnote   1 www.buildingbiology.co.uk (accessed on 19 January 2017).
Sources   ecodesign.co.uk
            rhs.org.uk
            RHS Rosemoor Project Profile
            http://www.ecodesign.co.uk/projects/culture-leisure/rosemoor
            Achim Pilz, Gale & Snowden Architects, Tomas Gartner, Wohnung + Gesundheit, 158, 3, 2016

The new building in Rosemoor provides classrooms,
a sheltered area for working outside next to
the learning garden facing south, as well as other
secondary rooms.

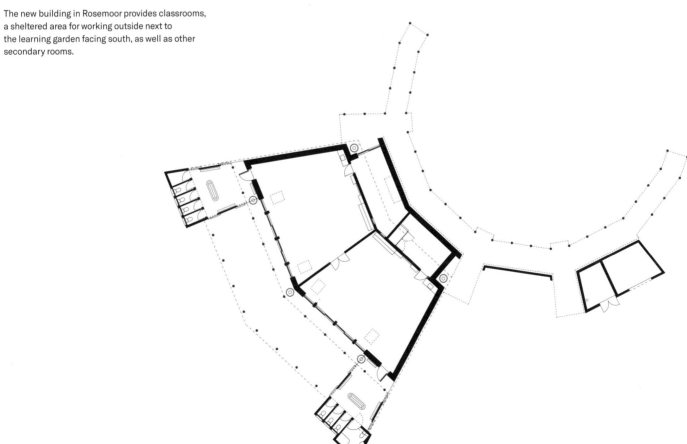

Floor plan, scale 1:400

In the entrance area, a projecting roof provides shelter on three sides and the continuation of the facade is like a welcoming embrace that encourages visitors to enter.

Site plan, scale 1:2000

Ecolino Daycare Center
Pfaffenhofen an der Ilm, Germany

The Ecolino Daycare Center is a public facility, which is part of the ecoQuartier urban expansion project in the town of Pfaffenhofen an der Ilm. Pfaffenhofen, a town that has implemented ambitious community climate protection and sustainability projects, paved the way for the ecoQuartier development, which began as a private initiative on former agricultural land at the Kramerbräuhof farm. Just as the farm was run according to ecological principles, this development is also committed to sustainability as well as the consistent implementation of building biology principles and the cradle-to-cradle concept. The mixed ecologically based residential, business, and agricultural use of the development is a key component of the concept for this district, establishing a symbiosis between the ecoQuartier development and the working farm. A circular economy is planned in which the farm provides a supporting function to the ecoQuartier in the form of supply and waste removal, heating energy from renewable energy sources, as well as wastewater and biowaste treatment. The principles of the ecoQuartier development are 100% committed to climate and resource protection, energy-efficient housing typologies, a well-balanced concept for open spaces, and a cross-generational sense of social connectedness in which childcare is both expected and required.

The ecoQuartier Ecolino Daycare Center is also a groundbreaking project for the municipality of Pfaffenhofen due to its ecological building approach and concept of inclusivity. It is a fully accessible facility and a role model for tolerance and equal opportunity with respect to the integration of those with individual disabilities and needs, regardless of their origin or religion.

Building biology was an essential part of the planning process right from the beginning: The site was assessed according to the Standard of Building Biology Testing Methods for geological disturbances, electric and magnetic fields, as well as gamma radiation. And a "Catalog of Building Biology- and Ecology-based Building Materials and Technologies" was also adhered to. For the freelance architect Rita Obereisenbuchner, the choice of simple, unprocessed building materials and a simplified building structure was the right path to ensure a high quality within the given budget.[1] The integrative character of the project is also evident in the simple architectural shape. In the entrance area, a projecting roof provides shelter on three sides and the continuation of the facade is like a welcoming embrace that encourages visitors to enter.

In keeping with the building biology-based building material and technology catalog, the daycare center was built as a wood-frame structure above ground level. Waterproof concrete is used where the structure has contact with the ground to prevent water penetration due to side hill seepage from the sandy clay soil of the sloped building site. Half of this floor is built into the slope and houses a multipurpose room, a meeting room, and learning spaces with open play areas. This basement level features foam glass insulation on the outside and an ad-

ditional layer of mineral insulation boards (calcium silicate hydrate) on the inside. The interior wall surfaces feature a clay plaster with a silicate-based finish that maintains the vapor permeability of the wall assembly and regulates the humidity level of the given space. The wood-frame construction on the ground level is also open to diffusion. Additionally, the combination of blown-in wood fiber insulation and wood fiber insulation boards as well as hemp insulation offers a well-balanced ratio of thermal storage and insulation capacity. To reveal the intrinsic characteristics of the building structure and material visually, stair surfaces and large interior surface areas are completed with untreated wood. For noise control, the combination of a suspended ceiling, which is made of wood slats filled with hemp insulation in the ceiling cavity, and wood fiberboards, which are fitted on acoustic elements, is another solution consistent with the building biology concept. All building materials were chosen to avoid the use of polystyrene, flame retardants, polyurethane, mineral wool, PVC, expanding foams, synthetic varnishes, isocyanates, and borates to also ensure safe and nontoxic conditions during installation and application.

With the goal to power the daycare center with 100% renewable energy, all the required electricity is generated by the photovoltaic system on the roof and the heating energy for the radiant floor heating system is provided by the district heating network fueled by wood chips. In the innermost rooms, fresh air is supplied by a mechanical ventilation system with heat recovery; in the main rooms, however, the optimum

air exchange is ensured by natural cross ventilation via motorized windows. By connecting the ventilation and heating systems with a KNX building control system, energy consumption can be reduced. And with the implementation of night-time cooling in summer, additional cooling efforts can be avoided. To counteract overheating in summer, the roof overhang and exterior blinds provide sufficient shading and the insulation features sufficient thermal storage capacity. To reduce the exposure to electromagnetic fields, DECT cordless phones and cell phones are not used and the children's sleeping areas are fitted with demand switches to de-energize the electrical wiring.

The water concept of the Ecolino Daycare Center has been integrated into the overall concept of the ecoQuartier development. The green roof serves as a buffer for rainwater whose infiltration is ensured across local retention areas. The wastewater piping network is designed for the use of gray water and constructed wetlands, once the entire ecoQuartier development has been completed. To maintain a high quality of drinking water, the daycare center opted for stainless steel piping consistent with the building biology recommendations.

In 2013, the Ecolino Daycare Center won the Fritz Bender Award for natural building. The jury acknowledged, in particular, the use of building materials recommended in building biology and the avoidance of toxins, the approach to recycling, as well as the ventilation and energy concept.

To reveal the intrinsic characteristics of the building structure and material visually, stair surfaces and large interior surface areas are completed with untreated wood.

Project	Ecolino Daycare Center
Architect	Architekturbüro Obereisenbuchner
Client	The City of Pfaffenhofen an der Ilm
Location	Pfaffenhofen an der Ilm, Germany
Completion	2013
Gross floor area	1126 m²
Construction cost	2,894,000 EUR (basement level 200–700)
Efficiency standard / certification	EnEV 2009
Annual heating energy demand	50.20 kWh/m²a
Annual primary energy demand	39.90 kWh/m²a
U-value exterior wall	0.16 W/m²K
U-value roof	0.10 W/m²K
Award	Fritz Bender Award 2013

Endnote   1 Achim Pilz, "Interview with Rita Obereisenbuchner," Wohnung + Gesundheit, 154, 1, 2015, p. 11
Sources   architekturbuero-obereisenbuchner.de
           pfaffenhofen.de/nachhaltigkeitspreis/
           ecoquartier.de
           Fritz-bender-stiftung.de/derbaupreis.htm
           Verena Schlegel, "Ecoquartier Pfaffenhofen," Wohnung + Gesundheit, 149, 4, 2013
           Achim Pilz, "Kindertagesstätte Ecolino," Wohnung + Gesundheit, 154, 1, 2015

Ground floor

Floor plans, scale 1:400

Upper floor

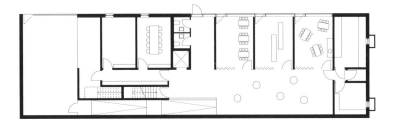

The simple, rectangular mass timber structure features a wall of glazing overlooking the inner courtyard, which provides additional views and perspectives from and to the spaces surrounding it to expand the children's world of experience.

Site plan, scale 1:2000

Pollenfeld Daycare Center
Pollenfeld, Germany

In 2011, the small municipality of Pollenfeld in Upper Bavaria announced an invited competition for the design of a children's daycare center with two group rooms. The proposal submitted by Kühnlein Architektur, an architectural firm based in the nearby municipality of Berching, won the competition with a timber structure to be built in the existing orchard. The architectural firm is a cross-generational venture that distinguishes itself with its focus on holistic design solutions. Its designs are ecological and sustainable. Humans are at the center of all design efforts. Nature serves as an invaluable resource. It is not surprising then that the architects chose only safe and ecological materials for the daycare center. They employed simple design principles and incorporated detailed solutions from an early stage to stay within the budget constraints of the public building. This project features many aspects of building biology. Since children—like the elderly, those in need, or the ill—require our special care, the implementation of building biology principles is especially pertinent here. Children rely on an uncontaminated environment for their immune and detoxification systems to develop normally and without any problems. Furthermore, they learn by grasping things, and this affinity for touch brings them into direct contact with surfaces that may expose them to harmful substances.

The siting of the Pollenfeld daycare center shows the architects' sensitive approach to location. The orchard and its old fruit trees were preserved. The courtyard, which opens toward the orchard, offers views served. The courtyard, which opens toward the orchard, offers views into nature. As an alternative to the orchard, the interior courtyard is another open space that invites children to explore. The simple, rectangular mass timber structure features a wall of glazing overlooking the inner courtyard, which offers additional views and perspectives from and to the spaces surrounding it. The group rooms at the ends on either side of the courtyard open to the outdoors, establishing a connection between the inside and outside across large format glazing. To protect the indoor spaces with the generous glazing from overheating in summer, the architects used horizontal blinds running the length of the interior facade facing south, creating a playful, semipermeable transition between the building structure and the open sky. The exterior wall is insulated with wood fiber insulation boards and completed with a rhombus profile siding made of weather-resistant, untreated larch strips. In contrast, the larch window frames received an oil finish. Over time, the untreated facade will develop a silver-gray patina as the natural weathering process forms a protective layer on the wood. Mass timber construction using cross-laminated timber panels is a great choice in terms of building biology, especially if a nontoxic adhesive (preferably white glue) is used. The wood-frame partition walls are filled with wood fiber, sheathed with natural fiberboard, and finished with lime plaster, which results in a wall assembly that is open to diffusion and hygroscopic as recommended in building biology. To control the noise in the daycare center, the acoustic ceilings are made of solid wood from silver fir with wood fiber insulation in the ceiling cavity to absorb the noise.

The facade is completed with a rhombus profile siding made of weather-resistant, untreated larch strips. Over time, the untreated facade will develop a silver-gray patina as the natural weathering process forms a protective layer on the wood.

The floor slab insulation with crushed recycled glass and the stainless steel roofing are both great choices in terms of building biology. Non-magnetic stainless steel is one of the few metals that does not distort the Earth's magnetic field. It also provides shielding against radio-frequency radiation. The roof is fitted with a gradient insulation made of wood fiber that provides thermal insulation against both winter and summer conditions. The layer of crushed brick underneath the extensive green area on the roof serves as another heat buffer and helps retain rainwater.

The single-level structure is a successful example of showcasing the simplicity of its materials. The surfaces children can reach are made of natural materials such as clay plaster, linoleum, and the exposed structural panels made of pure wood. The natural surfaces have a positive impact on indoor climate. The lime plaster does not require any additional finishing and also has a great sorption capacity, while the linoleum is free of hazardous substances such as PVC. The wood surfaces are untreated, as are the custom-made solid wood furnishings with their oil or wax finish. With regard to the electroclimate, static electricity will most likely not build up on those surfaces.

With a connection to the local district heating network of the neighboring primary school, the daycare center also enjoys a renewable energy source for heating in the form of wood chips. The low-temperature floor heating system provides natural radiant heat at floor level where the one- to three-year-old children need it the most. For health reasons, the maximum surface temperature should not exceed 23 °C. A conscious effort was made to keep building technologies at a minimum. There is no mechanical ventilation system. Instead, trickle vents were integrated into the exterior wall assembly to provide cross ventilation for optimized natural ventilation.

For artificial lighting, fluorescent tubes were chosen. The mercury content and potential fluctuations in the brightness of the lamp, so-called flicker, were taken into account. Flicker is a stress factor that can negatively influence neural processes in the body. According to building biology criteria, artificial lighting should match sunlight and daylight as closely as possible, be flicker-free, offer a continuous color spectrum, and feature a good color rendering index (CRI > 90).

The surfaces children can reach are made of natural
materials such as clay plaster, linoleum,
and the exposed structural panels made of pure wood.
The natural surfaces have a positive impact
on indoor climate.

Project	Pollenfeld Daycare Center
Architect	Kühnlein Architektur
Client	Municipality of Pollenfeld
Location	Pollenfeld, Germany
Completion	August 2013
Gross floor area	323 m², usable are 260 m²
Construction cost	1,000,000 EUR (basement level 200-700)
Efficiency standard / certification	EnEV 2009 -84%
Annual heating energy demand	95.25 kWh/m²a
Annual primary energy demand	34.00 kWh/m²a
U-value exterior wall	0.16 W/m²K
U-value roof	0.12 W/m²K
Award	Architektouren 2014

Sources   kuehnlein-architektur.de
           Susanne Kreykenbohm, "Nähe zum Detail," DBZ, 5, 2016
           dbz.de/artikel/dbz_Naehe_zum_Detail_Kinderkrippe_Pollenfeld_2566461.html

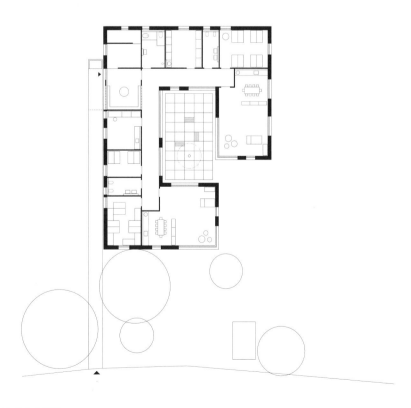

Floor plans, scale 1:400

Herbafarm—a farm located in the district of Bodrum—
specializes in organic farming based on the principles
of permaculture. So it seemed logical to design and
build the new structures—carefully nestled into the
lush vegetation—by following the principles of building
biology.

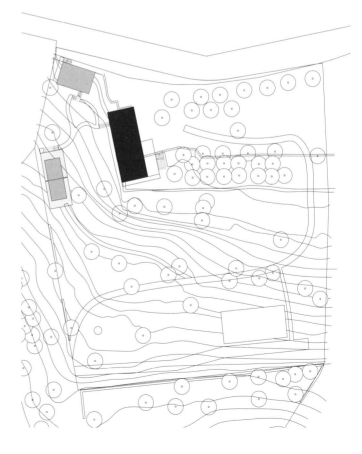

Site plan, scale 1:1000

Herbafarm
Bodrum, Turkey

Herbafarm—a farm located in the district of Bodrum on the southwest coast of Turkey by the Aegean Sea—specializes in organic farming based on the principles of permaculture. Bill Mollison and David Holmgren coined the term permaculture—a combination of "permanent" and "agriculture"—in the 1970s to describe, "an integrated, evolving system of perennial or self-perpetuating plant and animal species useful to humans."[1] The concept offers a whole-systems thinking informed by ethics and design principles to develop ways of life that make it possible to fulfill today's needs locally and improve the conservation of nature for future generations.[2]

Apart from regional fruit and vegetables, olives, herbs, as well as medicinal plants, carob trees are the main crop at Herbafarm in the mountains near the city of Bodrum overlooking the Aegean Sea. With a background in pharmacy, the farm operator uses her knowledge of natural and medicinal herbs to offer courses in herbal medicine and permaculture. So it seemed logical to design and build the new structures necessary for the operation of the holistic farm by following the principles of building biology. A guesthouse with separate bedrooms and a garden house were built, both of which were carefully nestled into the lush vegetation. The master plan developed by the architects And Akman and Mehmet Şenol of eds+ architects also includes a third building that is currently being designed to house social facilities and a residential unit. And Akman is the founder of Yapı Biyolojisi & Ekolojisi Enstitüsü (YBE),[3] the Turkish institute of building biology,

a partner of the Institute of Building Biology + Sustainability IBN in Rosenheim, Germany.

The guesthouse consists of two bedrooms with their own bathrooms and separate entrances. The two units are shaped in such a way that they emulate the terraced landscape. The garden house is on the same level and includes a bedroom and a living and dining space with an open kitchen unit. The wood-frame buildings feature projecting elements and wooden slats around the glazing to provide shade. To withstand the local climate—hot summers, but cold, wet winters—the buildings were insulated. Both on the roof and on the base plate, a layer of loose perlite was installed over tongue-and-groove formwork or marine grade plywood, respectively.

Due to the sloped site and the often extreme precipitation in winter and spring, the building is set 300 mm above the ground so that rainwater can drain away and moisture cannot rise up from below. The exterior walls feature reed insulation and the windows thermal insulation glazing so that no additional heating is required for the mostly sunny days in winter. There is no need for air conditioning in summer thanks to the shading elements and the cooling effect of cross ventilation at night.

The environmental performance of the building
is good because industrially produced
wood products were not used. All dimensional
lumber is domestic spruce and was cut
and assembled on site.

Project	Herbafarm
Architect	eds+ architects, ecological design solutions
Client	Meltem Kurtsan
Location	Bodrum, Muğla Province, Turkey
Completion	2016
Gross floor area	127 m²
Construction cost	65,000 EUR
Efficiency standard / certification	EnEV for Existing Building
Annual heating energy demand	Heating energy demand: guesthouse 20 kWh/m²a, garden house 17 kWh/m²a
Annual primary energy demand	109 kWh/m²a
U-value exterior wall	0.3 W/m²K
U-value roof	0.3 W/m²K

Endnotes 1 Bill Mollison and David Holmgren, Permaculture One, Tasmania, Australia: Tagari Publications, 1978
        2 David Holmgren, Das Wesen der Permakultur, permacultureprinciples.com/resources/free-downloads/ (accessed on 18 January 2017)
        3 YBE-yapibiyolojisi.org/homepage (accessed on 18 January 2017)
Sources eds-a.com
        Türkisches Institut für Baubiologie + Ökologie, Wohnung + Gesundheit, 157, 4, 2015

Guesthouse

Garden house

Floor plans, scale 1:250

The environmental performance of the building is good because industrially produced wood products were not used. All dimensional lumber is domestic spruce from a regional supplier and was cut and assembled on site, including the diagonal board sheathing for reinforcement.

Materials recommended by building biology were also used for the interior. Furthermore, ingredients were screened for chemical additives. Cellulose panels with cradle-to-cradle certification were selected for the interior surfaces of both the exterior and partition walls. These panels are made of recycled materials, can be composted, and are nontoxic. They do not contain adhesives since the cellulose fibers are pressed into panels using pressure and heat only. Natural paints were used to finish panel surfaces in the sleeping and living areas. Visible wood surfaces such as ceilings, windows, and doors were soaped, and the floor received a wax finish. Thus the interior surfaces remain open to diffusion and hygroscopic, which promotes a healthy indoor climate and helps regulate air humidity. In the wet rooms, cement-bonded boards were installed, which were also finished with natural paints.

With regard to building services technology, only the bare minimum was installed. The drinking water pipes are made of stainless steel for hygienic reasons. The fresh water for the entire complex comes from the rainwater collected to feed the garden irrigation system and from the farm well for the domestic water, so the farm is independent from the local water supply. To also become self-sufficient with regard to electricity, a photovoltaic system is planned for the third building yet to be built. The wiring in the various buildings is completed following the principles of building biology. The sleeping areas are free of electrical wiring to minimize the exposure to ELF electric and magnetic fields. Owing to the simple structural shapes, conscious choice of materials, and careful placement, the Herbafarm buildings blend well into the natural surroundings. The Herbafarm complex is one of the first pilot projects of the building biology movement in Turkey.

The staggered alignment of the rooms, which follows the terrain, demonstrates the unusual but sensitive approach chosen by the architects for the site. The rural image of Hohenbercha is reflected in the barn-like shape of the new guesthouse and carried forward into today's world.

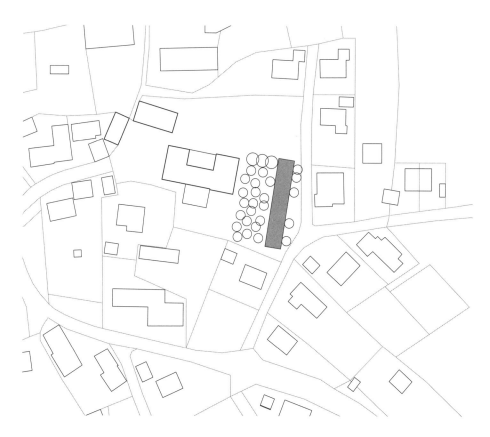

Site plan, scale 1:2000

Hörger Biohotel Tafernwirtschaft
Hohenbercha, Germany

The German "Tafernrecht," or tavern's right to serve, is evoked in the name of the Hörger Biohotel Tafernwirtschaft, which has been in the hands of the Hörger family for the past 125 years. In 1998, the current generation's spirit of innovation led to a change in the management of the hotel based exclusively on organic and ecological principles. In 2006 then, this holistic approach combined with the historical roots and relationships this hotel has with the town, led to the construction of a guesthouse following ecological and biological criteria. "The aim here … is to show that sustainability does not mean abstinence. Instead, the purest natural products … make a major contribution to the quality of life."[1] For one thing, the design by Deppisch Architects shows the hotel's local roots; for another, it displays the modernity of the times—all brought together in an aesthetic, contemporary architecture.

The rural image of Hohenbercha is reflected in the barn-like shape of the new guesthouse and carried forward into today's world—without denying its relation to the farming structures in the region. The historical fruit tree garden, with its old apple trees going back to the time of "Apple Pastor" Korbinian Aigner, was preserved and is now the centerpiece of the newly created ensemble, which consists of the main building, natural garden, and guesthouse wing. The barn-like character of the new guesthouse is defined by its proportions and the darkly stained larch slats of the arbor. The staggered alignment of the rooms, which follows the terrain, demonstrates the unusual but sensitive approach chosen by the architects for the site.

The building is a mass timber structure (cross-laminated) made of stone pine. The prefabricated room units were uncoupled from one another, stacked and aligned in just two weeks. This modular, staggered layout of the structure also helped meet the German sound insulation standards (DIN), both by calculation and after installation.

There were a number of reasons to choose stone pine. The health benefits of this material, especially for sleep, have been established in studies by Johanneum Research in Austria. According to one study, stone pine has positive effects on human endurance and recovery. "This expresses itself in a lower heart rate during physical or mental stress situations and following rest phases and/or during an accelerated autonomic recovery process."[2] The study further states that stone pine leads to improved quality of sleep and that it has a beneficial effect on our moods throughout the day, making us more sociable. The insecticidal and antibacterial effects of stone pine oil have also been proven. With its positive impact on indoor climate, stone pine also helps those who feel under the weather, since it improves indoor air quality and indoor air pressure.[3] In the Biohotel, the untreated natural wood surfaces are open to diffusion and hygroscopic, contributing to a comfortable indoor climate.

The sustainability of the selected building
materials is evident in the insulation
materials from renewable, recycled raw materials
such as wood fiber and cellulose.

Project	Hörger Biohotel
Architect	Deppisch Architects
Client	Hörger Biohotel Tafernwirtschaft
Location	Hohenbercha, Germany
Completion	July 2006
Gross floor area	589 m², usable area 461 m²
Construction cost	1,811,990 EUR (basement level 100–700)
Efficiency standard / certification	EnEV 2004
Annual heating energy demand	Heating energy demand 50 kWh/m²a
Annual primary energy demand	Information not available
U-value exterior wall	0.19 W/m²K
U-value roof	0.17 W/m²K
Awards	Tourismus Architektur Preis 2011
	European Architecture Award Energy + Architecture 2011
	BDA Preis Bayern 2010
	Deutscher Holzbaupreis Anerkennung 2009
	[German Wood Construction Award, Honorary Mention]

Endnotes   1 hoerger-biohotel.de/hoerger-biohotel/philosophie-geschichte/ (accessed on 23 January 2017)
2 Joanneum Research, Stone Pine: Positive Health Effects of Stone Pine Furniture, PDF summary, p. 2
3 Documentary: Gesundes Holz, Zirbe aus Kärnten, ORF 2013
Sources   deppischarchitekten.de
Baunetzwissen.de, gesund bauen, Bio-Hotel in Hohenbercha, Gästehaus mit ökologischem Kontext
Baunetzwissen.de, Heizung, Bio-Hotel in Hohenbercha, Biomasse-Nahwärme, Abluft-WRG für Brauchwasser und Photovoltaik
Hoerger-biohotel.de/hoerger-biohotel/

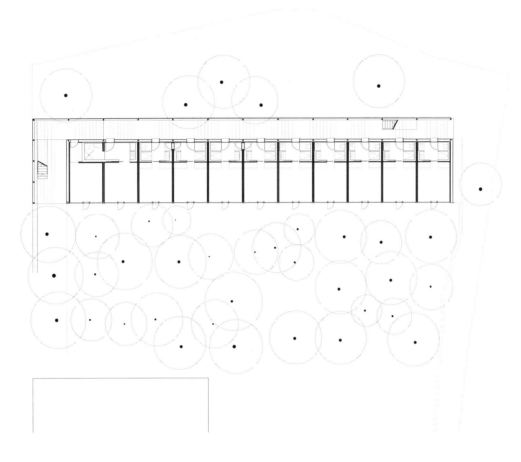

The sustainability of the selected building materials is not only evident in the stone pine, which is locally available in the Alps, but also in the insulation materials from renewable, recycled raw materials such as wood fiber and cellulose.

The western facade of the guesthouse opens to the apple orchard with large glazing panels using triple insulating panes to keep the heat loss low. In winter, these rooms benefit from passive solar heat gains; in summer, the fruit trees provide shade. Furthermore, capillary-like, light-scattering structures integrated into the glazing refract the incoming light, creating an artistic play of light and shadow that contributes to the guests' relaxation during the later hours of the day. Maximizing the amount of daylight exposure reduces the need for artificial lighting, which is supplied by energy-efficient LED technology. The low-temperature floor heating system in the solid oak parquet produces a pleasant radiant heat that has a positive effect on surface temperatures and, by extension, indoor climate. Through a connection to the biomass district heating network of the local municipality, the heating energy requirements are met with a renewable energy source. Another decentralized renewable energy source is the building-integrated photovoltaic system embedded at roof level. The photovoltaic system was sized to cover the additional electricity requirements of the guesthouse and therefore also covers the requirements of the extension.

A sustainable symbiosis between the new and the existing building is also found in the hot water system, whereby the waste heat of the cooling system in the existing building is used via a heat exchanger to heat the hot water in the new building. The water pipes are completed in stainless steel for hygiene reasons.

An integral way of thinking also lies at the heart of other design areas. All installations were integrated into the prefabricated structural wood panels during manufacture. ThermoWood, a thermally modified wood, was used to ensure the flexible use of the bedroom access areas as both a bathroom and an entrance hall. A decentralized ventilation system with trickle vents along the window frames combined with an exhaust air system in the sanitary area provides for a natural air exchange. A low-EMF electric system was achieved by implementing a star-like wiring layout to the individual rooms and by installing a hardwired Wi-Fi network to avoid exposure to RF radiation. Finally, the rainwater is collected from the slanted roof on the southern end of the building where it can flow freely into a neighboring creek, bringing life to the flora and fauna of the surrounding area.

The Almrefugio is the result of converting
an old hay and cow barn into a four-star hotel.
The existing structures were renovated
in a sustainable manner using natural and
ecological building materials.

Site plan, scale 1:2000

Almrefugio
Neumarkt, Upper Palatinate, Germany

The Almrefugio, in the Höhenberg neighborhood of Neumarkt in the Upper Palatinate region of Germany, is the result of converting an old hay and cow barn into a four-star hotel. Berschneider + Berschneider Architects renovated the existing structures in a sustainable manner using natural and ecological building materials. The hotel is now organized on two levels. The guest rooms are on the upper floor and some of the rooms feature a loft, thereby making full use of the space provided by the roof structure. The reception is on the ground floor, along with a small bar and an apartment offering barrier-free access.

After carefully cleaning the timber structure, the architectural team decided to leave the surfaces untreated. So the original timber structure of the existing buildings remained intact; it was strengthened and changed only where necessary. Thanks to the new roof design, the loft remains part of the building experience. On the ground floor, the existing plaster was removed from the quarry stone wall, which was then cleaned before being repointed with lime mortar. Traces of the past can be found throughout the structure of the repurposed building; the guest rooms even feature old feeding and drinking troughs. An old hay crane hangs suspended in the open space of the stairwell and the structure's former use as a cow barn becomes clear with the image displayed on the hallway ceiling. Since local carpenters made many of the new fittings, the cast-iron elements of the old barn could be reused as handles on the furniture, doors, and windows. Newly added materials are chosen for their natural features and ecology.

The new roof installed over the existing roof framework is fitted on the inside with three-layer cross-laminated timber made of spruce whose coating of linseed oil leaves it open to diffusion. Behind this planking, the new roof is insulated with rock wool. As a rule, insulation made of renewable raw materials has a better environmental performance and better humidity-buffering properties, which led to the use of permeable wood fiber insulation boards on the outside. The good thermal properties of the natural insulation boards are also an advantage in terms of protection against summer overheating. The hotel rooms feature health-certified solid oak parquet flooring finished with natural oils. Though the oil finish reduces the open-pore structure of the wood surface, it also increases its durability consistent with the use in the hotel. In the reception area, the solid oak parquet flooring is made of discarded railroad ties, which were tested for harmful substances and found to be free of toxins before they were cleaned and finished with soap. Their worn, wind-beaten appearance bears witness to their former use. Other floors were finished using lime putty.

All interior plaster wall surfaces are finished with lime plaster, which provides the necessary regulation of indoor air humidity. Layers of lime plaster were applied in different ways to the load-bearing masonry walls, either by a mechanical plastering machine or roughly troweled by hand to give the surfaces a varied appearance. A transparent coat of dispersion paint was used to make the textures visible. The partition walls of the hallway and rooms on the upper level were constructed

using dry construction methods and soundproofed in compliance with DIN standards. An ecologically safe silicate paint with natural pigments was chosen for finishing the walls. Finishes based on lime or silicate are fully vapor permeable. For the purpose of soundproofing, a carpet made of pure maize fiber runs along the hallway. When choosing carpeting, the principles of building biology recommend that no harmful substances are emitted such as plasticizers from synthetic backing materials, mothproofing agents, or flame retardants.

The heating system of the new guest wing in the hay barn is connected to the one at the existing inn to save costs. This heating supply is supported by a photovoltaic system so that the low-temperature floor heating system in the reception area and the sanitary areas can be powered with renewable energy. The rooms are also equipped with quickly adjustable flat panel radiators that offer a high level of radiant heat. When a room is vacant and unused, the temperature can be quickly lowered thanks to the quick response time of the system. A building component temperature control embedded in the newly cast concrete base of the quarry stone wall serves as an additional source of heat. Thus the masonry walls not only emit comfortable radiant heat, but at the same time help dry any moisture rising through the capillaries of the wall.

For the electrical installation, a star-like wiring layout was chosen to reduce exposure to power-frequency electric and magnetic fields.

The use of a hardwired network ensures low exposure levels to radio-frequency (RF) radiation in the workplace. RF radiation from Wi-Fi antennas can be further reduced by the orientation and location of the transmitting antennas, as well as the choice of frequency ranges. The distortion of the Earth's magnetic field due to the structural steel strengthening of the old wood beam ceiling is equalized by the fact that any bed surface is at a safe distance of about 500 mm. The rooms have natural ventilation and the shower areas are equipped with individual exhaust fans to ensure the direct removal of moisture.

The interior lighting concept and handcrafted furniture create a pleasant atmosphere. In addition to floor lamps, antique lamps provide indirect lighting for the wall surfaces and roof timbers. The wrought iron support for the washstands along with the signage showcase the craftsmanship of regional companies that were closely involved in the design process with the architects.

On the ground floor, the existing plaster was
removed from the quarry stone wall,
which was then cleaned before being repointed
with lime mortar.

Project	Almrefugio
Architect	Berschneider + Berschneider
Client	Landgasthaus Almhof
Location	Neumarkt in der Oberpfalz, Upper Palatinate, Germany
Completion	June 2015
Gross floor area	Usable area 353 m²
Construction cost	1,150,000 EUR (basement level 200–700)
Efficiency standard / certification	Meets EnEV 2014 for building components
Annual heating energy demand	Information not available
Annual primary energy demand	Information not available
U-value exterior wall	0.19 W/m²K
U-value roof	0.21 W/m²K
Award	People's Choice Award "geplant + ausgeführt" 2016

Sources   berschneider.com
           Das Heustadel-Hotel, Deutsche Handwerkszeitung, 11 March 2016

An old hay crane still hangs suspended in the open space of the stairwell. Thanks to the new roof design, the old roof trusses remain part of the building experience.

Ground floor

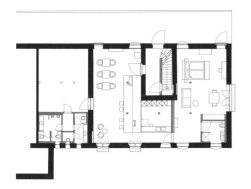

First upper floor

Second upper floor

Floor plans, scale 1:400

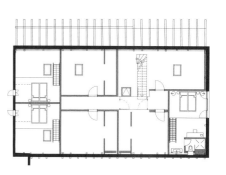

In Margreid in Italy, Casa Salute GmbH built its company headquarters—including a showroom, a company apartment, and a model apartment—strictly in line with the principles of building biology.

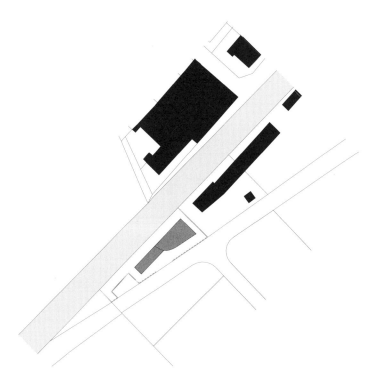

Site plan, scale 1:2000

Casa Salute
Margreid, South Tyrol, Italy

In Margreid an der Weinstraße in the province of Bolzano-Bozen (Italy), Casa Salute GmbH built its company headquarters—including a showroom, a company apartment, and a model apartment—strictly in line with building biology principles and methods. The company has promoted products of mass timber construction since 2002. The aim is to build healthy, ecological, energy-efficient buildings for the future. Together with the architect Marco Sette, the owners of the company, Herta Peer and Klaus Romen, developed their new headquarters in 2012 as an ensemble consisting of a two-level building and a single-level guesthouse for clients to experience living in a mass timber structure.

The main building breaks down into an office level with an exhibition and lecture space on the ground floor and a residential level on the upper floor, whose terrace extends over the guesthouse as a roof. On the elongated property, the two buildings are stacked in a row, while both feature large glazing areas facing south toward the sun. The projecting elements of the terrace on the upper level provide protection from the sun. As a result, the rooms are flooded with light, but also have sufficient shade in summer and, in winter, they still receive the warmth of the sun. The building does not have many openings to the north; however, they are aligned in such a way that they afford selective views of the landscape. On the ground level, the spaces for auxiliary functions also serve as a buffer zone to the north.

The building structure was completed with solid timber harvested from certified forests. The mass timber elements were manufactured without the use of adhesives. This guarantees the high reutilization value of this building material over its entire life cycle. The mass timber elements made of softwood have multiple layers of cross-laminated solid wood strips (horizontal, diagonal, vertical), which are then connected with hardwood screws. This connection ensures the required dimensional and structural stability. The fire protection standards (DIN) can be achieved by the selection of a single material that forms an insulating layer of charcoal, which slows down the spread of fire. The sound insulation standards (DIN) can also be met because of the sound-absorbing properties of mass timber construction. A layer of wood fiber insulation boards gives the commercial building the required thermal insulation and wind resistance. The tongue-and-groove connections and crosswise pattern of installation ensure that the building envelope is windproof. The wall assembly remains vapor permeable, and the use of solid materials prevents thermal bridges, thereby eliminating the risk of condensation and mold growth. On the exterior, the commercial building uses materials that have an open-pore structure. The untreated larch siding and the lime plaster keep the exterior walls open to diffusion.

Ergonomically designed built-in furnishings
and furniture are custom-made
without the use of adhesives or varnishes.

The choice of materials for the interior was also based on aspects of optimal energy efficiency and ecology, on criteria of healthy indoor air and how they affect human health. In addition to the structural mass timber interior walls, wood fiberboard panels and lime plaster were used for the ceiling and untreated larch for the flooring. Since these materials are vapor permeable and hygroscopic, they have a positive impact on indoor climate. Furthermore, a suspended ceiling at ground level adds to the sound insulation on the upper level and also functions as an installation cavity. Together with the lime plaster, the wood fiberboard panels regulate the air humidity and also absorb sound. The ceiling is fitted with capillary tube mats that provide radiant heating and cooling as needed. The interior walls with a clay plaster finish provide additional heating surfaces.

Physiological as well as psychological aspects were considered for the interior design. Ergonomically designed built-in furnishings and furniture are custom-made without the use of adhesives or varnishes. Geomantic measurements were carried out on the property to assess the Earth's magnetic field, underground watercourses, and radio-frequency radiation (microwaves, radio waves). To avoid electromagnetic stress, the findings were incorporated into the building design. The densely reinforced concrete foundation slab, for example, was completely covered with a spacing layer of brick to avoid distortions of the Earth's magnetic field in the living space by establishing more distance between the steel reinforcement and the flooring level. The foundation slab itself rests on a layer of crushed limestone and foam glass. For low-EMF wiring, shielded cables and receptacles were used. Additionally, the circuits for the bedrooms were equipped with demand switches to be able to de-energize the wiring in the sleeping areas. A building automation system with wireless control switches also helps to reduce the spread of electromagnetic fields. These switches make use of the "energy harvesting" principle, whereby the motion energy, released while pressing the switch, is harvested to send a radio signal to the receiver. Research shows that this type of wireless switch emits significantly lower levels of RF radiation (compared with a standard wired light switch) and, by extension, electrosmog.[1] Work spaces are equipped with hardwired connections and access to wireless (Wi-Fi) applications is not provided. Shielding curtains were used to protect against radio-frequency radiation from the outside. Shielding lime plasters can also be used.[2] Artificial lighting is provided by flicker-free halogen and LED lamps.

The building is self-sufficient as far as energy is concerned. The heating and cooling energy as well as the electricity are supplied by a photovoltaic thermal hybrid solar system (electricity/warm water) and a hybrid heat pump (air/water and water/water) including a buffer tank for heating, cooling, and domestic hot water. The on-site generated electricity also powers an electric vehicle charging station. A decentralized ventilation system for individual rooms ensures adequate air exchange, although it is mostly dealt with manually. Some of the were

The choice of materials for the interiors was also based
on aspects of optimal energy efficiency and
ecology, on criteria of healthy indoor air and how they
affect human health.

Project	Casa Salute
Architect	Studio M7 – Marco Sette
Client	Casa Salute GmbH, Herta Peer, Klaus Romen
Location	Margreid, South Tyrol, Italy
Completion	June 2013
Gross floor area	350 m²
Construction cost	825,000 EUR
Efficiency standard / certification	KlimaHaus Gold Nature (KlimaHaus Certification South Tyrol IT)
Annual heating energy demand	1794 kWh/a / 5.12 kWh/m²a
Annual primary energy demand	9700 kWh/a / 27.71 kWh/m²a (measured consumption)
U-value exterior wall	0.13 W/m²K
U-value roof	0.12 W/m²K
Award	KlimaHaus Gold Nature

Endnotes   1 Martin H. Virnich, "Tasterfunk," Wohnung + Gesundheit, 162, 1, 2017
              2 P. Pauli, D. Moldan, Reduzierung hochfrequenter Strahlung im Bauwesen: Baustoffe und Abschirmmaterialien, 3rd ed., Fürth: AnBUS, 2015, p. 72f
Sources   casa-salute.it
              m-7.it/Riviste.pdf
              Mechela Toni, CasaClima Awards 2014, i vincitori: Casa Salute a Magre, architetto.info
              Film on the project: Casa Salute, Ein Haus im Sinne der Natur, youtube.com
              Marc-Wilhelm Lennartz und Susanne Jacob-Freitag, Neues Bauen mit Holz, Basel: Birkhäuser Verlag, 2015
              Marc-Wilhelm Lennartz, "Casa Salute – das gesunde Haus," Wohnung + Gesundheit 150, 1, 2014

copper, which does not pose a risk for commercial use and adult users. To avoid heavy metal exposure, stainless steel or galvanized copper can be used. For those pipes where the water is not used for human consumption, PEX piping was chosen.

Rainwater is collected and used for irrigation purposes. The site itself makes seepage possible via gravel and green surfaces. The casement window element with triple-glazed low-iron oxide glass panels (without insulating foil) is a building science experiment; however, there is another glass pane on the inside at a distance of 180 mm. The idea behind this is to profit from solar gains in winter despite the triple-glazed panel. To test the efficacy of this set-up, measurements were taken over a period of one year. In 2014, the Casa Salute was awarded the KlimaHaus Gold Nature certification for its heating energy requirement of 5.12 kWh/m²a. The effectively measured total primary energy requirement for the year from the summer of 2015 to the summer of 2016 was ultimately 25% below the level calculated by the KlimaHaus agency.

Ground floor

Upper floor

Scale 1:400

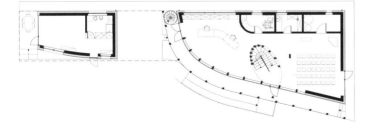

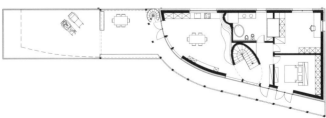

The commercial building of Artis GmbH—a wood engineering, consulting and interior construction company—is a successful commercial project that showcases how mixed use, densification, and neighborly relations can work organically in an urban setting.

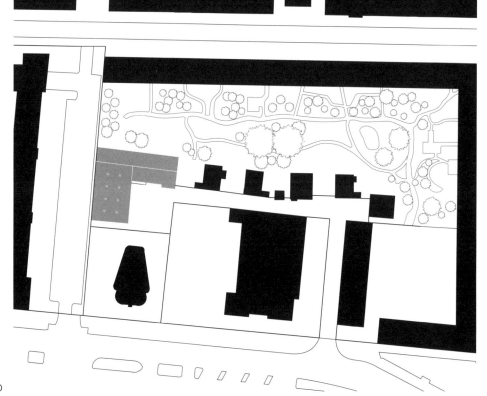

Site plan, scale 1:2000

Artis Commercial Building
Berlin, Germany

The commercial building of Artis GmbH—a wood engineering, consulting and interior construction company—is a successful commercial project that showcases how mixed use, densification, and neighborly relations can work organically in an urban setting. The Berlin architects and engineers Ziegert | Roswag | Seiler completed this project for one of their contracting companies. The Artis project shows how it is possible to create a commercial building based on the principles of building biology. As a preventive discipline, building biology is at its most effective in areas worth protecting the most, such as rest and sleep environments, but its preventive effects can also be brought to bear on everyday work environments.

The new complex is grouped around an inbound delivery and access zone in an L-shaped configuration. It consists of a single-level production hall with a wood shingle siding and a visually offset administration building, which is insulated with a renewable insulation material and finished with a mineral-based plaster. The latter houses the design, administration, and staff areas on the upper level. The production hall connects to the bench area for further manufacturing processes, as well as the paint shop and outbound delivery area, creating a transparent production process. This transparency of the production process on the ground level continues with the visual connection between administration and production, leading to work spaces defined by a sense of community as well as cooperation that foster good working conditions.

The commercial building is a wood structure that meets low-energy construction standards (86% below EnEV 2009) and is built with renewable natural building materials. Mass timber wood products such as cross-laminated timber, also as ceiling elements, were used for the structure, while three-layer panels were used for the interior design. The highly insulating building envelope made of wood fiber and cellulose, which achieves transmission heat losses well below the German Energy Saving Ordinance from 2009 (EnEV), made it possible to use more energy-efficient systems for the building services and equipment.

The elements of the timber construction were sized to meet the F30 fire protection requirements; only the paint shop, which required an F90 B-compliant partition, was completed with a double layer of gypsum fiberboard on the inside to obtain approval. Conventional XPS polystyrene insulation boards were placed underneath the foundation slab and OSB panels were used to stiffen the timber panels. In building biology, foam glass insulation and diagonal wood sheathing would be recommended here. When making a building biology assessment of wood products with adhesives, those with formaldehyde emissions should be ruled out, if possible. In the case of elevated concentration levels of pollutants and formaldehyde in indoor air, it is important to install a ventilation system that can provide the necessary air exchange or to use wood products that are made with nontoxic adhesives (e.g. PVA or white glue) in the first place.

The work spaces are defined by a sense
of community, supporting cooperation
and good working conditions.

The indoor climate in the commercial building profits from the use of clay plaster on wood fiberboard panels in the office wing, which has a high sorption capacity, and the use of untreated structural wood and interior wood surfaces with a wax finish. The good thermal storage capacity of renewable insulation materials such as wood fiberboard and cellulose offers exceptional summer heat protection and thus prevents overheating. This continues in the administration area with a green roof, which also improves the microclimate of the surrounding area. The high degree of prefabrication of the wood elements leads to barely detectable levels of moisture in the new building, which has a positive effect on interior surface temperatures. This is also supported by the radiant heat supplied through the various heating surfaces in the production hall and the floor heating zones in the offices, which can be individually controlled for each room.

The required heating energy for the heating, air-conditioning, and ventilation systems is provided by a condensing solid fuel boiler, using shredded waste wood from their own production. Two buffer storage tanks are connected in series, providing all the hot water (heating, ventilation, hot water) required to run the entire facility self-sufficiently. The combination of a highly efficient control technology for the ventilation system, including special provisions for the paint shop, as well as the use of a highly efficient waste heat recovery system, made it possible for the entire facility to be operated without any additional heat source. Large portions of the operational electricity are generated by the photovoltaic system mounted on the roof of the production hall, which is a decentralized source of renewable energy. When in basic operation mode, the building even becomes an energy-plus house and generates a surplus. The engineers managed to reduce the complex technologies of the operation to a minimum by establishing a comprehensive and smart synchronization of all technical systems.

The openness of the project design also allows for the efficient use of daylight. For one thing, the large format glazing connecting the administration area is very conducive to lighting; for another, the production hall, whose walls cannot be fitted with openings for production and storage reasons, has skylights and a continuous light shelf for adequate daylighting.

The Artis commercial building won the 2016 Fritz Bender Award for natural building. This award was given in recognition of the recyclable, CO_2-neutral engineering wood construction in a mixed urban area, use of low-emission building materials, vapor-permeable building envelope, natural lighting, and high-quality design, especially with regard to the load-bearing structure with its fish belly trusses.[1]

On the ground floor, the production hall connects the
various functional areas, making the production
process transparent. This transparency of the production
process on the ground level continues with the
visual connection between administration and production.
The work spaces are defined by a sense of community
as well as cooperation.

Project	Artis Commerical Building
Architect	Ziegert I Roswag I Seiler
Client	Artis GmbH
Location	Berlin, Germany
Completion	January 2012
Gross floor area	1978 m², usable area 1565 m²
Construction cost	1,979,044 EUR (basement level 300 + 400)
Efficiency standard / certification	EnEV 2009 -50% (89%), Plus-energy House in basic operation mode
Annual heating energy demand	47.77 kWh/m²a
Annual primary energy demand	22.58 kWh/m²a
U-value exterior wall	0.12 W/m²K / production hall 0.15 W/m²K
U-value roof	0.13 W/m²K / production hall 0.15 W/m²K
Award	Fritz Bender Award 2016

Endnote   1 Cf. https://www.zrs-berlin.de/images/aktuelles/FBB/160625_Urkunde_Fritz-Bender-Preis2016.jpg (accessed on 19 March .2017)
Sources   zrs-berlin.de
             ZRS press kit 11/2012
             Fritz-bender-stiftung.de/derbaupreis.htm
             Film: Artis Firmensitz, Berlin – Gewerbebau – innerstädtisch und nachhaltig
             [Artis Headquarters, Berlin–Commercial Building, Sustainable Intraurban Construction]
             Christine Ryll, "Wenn der Kunde zum Kunden wird" [When the Client Turns Client], in: Mikado, 4, 2012

Ground floor

Upper floor

Floor plans, scale 1:750

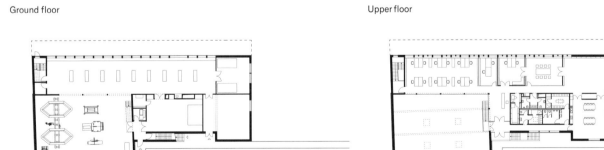

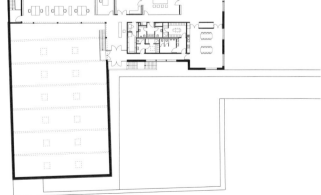

At the Omicron Campus, being able to use the building in varied and individual ways is seen as extremely important. The building creates the best possible work spaces to meet the needs of the employees.

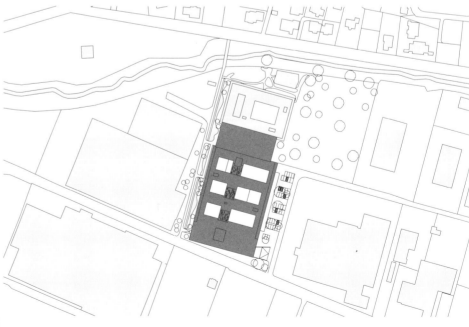

Site plan, scale 1:4000

Omicron Campus
Klaus, Austria

The way the coworkers communicate and meet is made a priority as can be seen in the layout of the open spaces and terraces, thinking spaces and hot spots.

Omicron Electronics GmbH can boast a long list of Austrian "Great Place to Work" awards. The company has earned recognition in ranking categories such as "Best Employer for Persons with Disabilities," "Best Employer for Holistic Health," or for reconciling the family-work balance. The latest award Omicron received was for "Best Employer 2016" among large companies in Austria.[1]

So it is not surprising that the extension designed by Dietrich | Untertrifaller Architects, which was opened in 2014 at the Omicron headquarters in the Vorarlberg town of Klaus (Austria), is a work environment where the employer takes the needs of its employees seriously. The Omicron Campus is a good example of how not only structural and energy-related, but also psychological, physiological, and landscape-related aspects can enhance a building in terms of building biology. Great efforts were made to accommodate the needs of the 200 employees in their everyday work environment. Thus the offices are variable office cubicles to address the desire for work spaces that allow for concentrated work. The way the employees communicate and meet is made a priority as can be seen in the layout of the open spaces and terraces, thinking zones and hot spots. All offices have a connection to the outside via projecting balconies and patios overlooking the Rhine valley. An access and recreation block in the middle of the building consolidates the meandering structure. This linear "ribbon" creates inner courtyards and provides unusual spatial experiences as well as hot spots that serve as oases to meet and relax. A three-dimensional

solid wood landscape by Georg Eichinger, which has an unusual way of connecting the floors with one another, invites the user to explore and experience space in different ways, as do the cave-like retreat and meeting cocoons made of clay by Anna Heringer and Martin Rauch. The relaxation areas round off the composition. All this contributes to a work environment that creates a sense of well-being and fosters creativity, performance, and collaboration among employees. At the same time, the commendable building biology choice of materials such as clay and wood provides for a pleasant indoor climate. The selected colors, staged lighting effects, and textiles create an atmosphere of contemplation and relaxation, thereby creating a stimulating contrast to the work spaces with their rigid structure of individual cubicles.

Being able to use the building in varied and individual ways is seen as extremely important. The offices, for example, are equipped with adjustable furniture to make alternative uses possible. To support optimal internal and external collaboration, the conscious decision was made to offer a wireless network for parts of the communication strategy; consequently, Wi-Fi coverage is available throughout the building. To reduce exposure to RF radiation, the wireless network design was optimized according to the motto "many transmitters—low power output" and the workstations were hardwired. To admit as much daylight as needed for the required levels of concentration, the partitions facing the hall and between office spaces are transparent from eye level.

To invite users to explore and experience space,
configurations like the cave-like retreat
and meeting cocoons made of clay by Anna Heringer
and Martin Rauch were created.

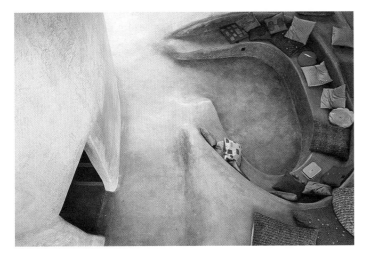

Through the ceiling-high glazing of the exterior facade, a maximum amount of daylight is available. As for the artificial lighting, individual control options are offered, so the lights can be adjusted to meet individual workplace needs. The low-flicker LED lamps can also be adjusted for light color and light intensity through the KNX building control system. The exterior solar controls shield against glare and also protect against overheating in summer. The cooling layer under wood paneling and acoustic absorbers made of renewable materials also help absorb internal loads.

The aim of the company was to demonstrate environmental awareness of energy and resources. Building materials were not only selected for being natural and regional, but their ingredients were also screened for being nontoxic. A building ecology consultant was contracted to assure both the quality of the building materials and their installation through appropriate construction management.

With regard to the load-bearing structure, a comparison of costs and CO_2 savings suggested reinforced concrete. Instead, the client decided to invest the budget in an ecological building method and a healthy interior design. So the building envelope was completed as a glass facade with a timber frame of local origin, the renewable insulation material was installed without the use of expanding foam, the surface of the oak flooring was roughly sawn, the custom-made partitions and furnishings were made of silver fir typical of the region, and the topcoat

of the clay plaster surfaces was bonded with casein. All of the above choices support a healthy and comfortable indoor climate.

The decision in favor of a low-impact energy supply was not only made to satisfy building code requirements, it was also a conscious choice. A geothermal pump and heat exchange technology supplies the building with the necessary heating and cooling performance. The required operational electricity is drawn from the photovoltaic system integrated into the facade of the storage building, which is located in front of the main building facing the street. In addition, an energy distribution system ensures the exchange of redundant energy between the building sections. The use of a demand-controlled ventilation system with heat recovery makes it possible again for employees to adjust the system to their individual needs.

With regard to the sociocultural context, it was important for Omicron to involve regional companies as well as local craftspeople. By collaborating with NGOs, which was facilitated through the company's commitment to Crossing Borders and Anna Heringer's work in India (Little Flower), it was possible to support aid projects and those in need. To compensate for the sealed surface area due to the new construction, a rooftop garden was set up that can also be used by the employees. The outer facilities were developed by the gardener Lothar Schmidt, who designed a landscape garden for local plant species some of which are threatened. This is yet another opportunity where a diverse flora and fauna can thrive.

The three-dimensional solid wood landscape by Georg Eichinger has an unusual way of making the various floors accessible.

Project	Omicron Campus
Architect	Dietrich	Untertrifaller Architects
Client	Omicron Electronics GmbH
Location	Klaus, Austria
Completion	December 2014
Gross floor area	12,770 m², usable area 11,300 m²
Construction cost	31,500,000 EUR
Efficiency standard / certification	Information not available
Annual heating energy demand	22 kWh/m²a
Annual primary energy demand	Information not available
U-value exterior wall	Glass facade: wooden frame 1.4 W/m²K, glass 0.6 W/m²K
U-value roof	0.13 W/m²K
Awards	Staatspreis Architektur Industrie und Gewerbe 2016
	Österreich bester Arbeitgeber 2016
	ZV Bauherrenpreis 2015
	Bester Arbeitgeber für ganzheitliche Gesundheitsförderung 2014
	Bester Arbeitgeber für Vereinbarung von Familie und Beruf 2012/2014
	Bester Arbeitgeber für Integration von Menschen mit Behinderung 2012

Endnote   1 greatworkplace.eu/rankings/oesterreichs-beste-arbeitgeber-2016 (accessed on 30 March 2017).
Sources   dietrich.untertrifaller.com
           anna-heringer.com
           Greatworkplace.eu/rankings/oesterreichs-beste-arbeitgeber-2016
           Sabine Blechschmidt, "Willkommen daheim," Kontur, Winter 2015
           Manuela Gatt, "Schreibtisch ersetzt Bett," Holzmagazin, 1, 2016
           Karin Tschavkova, "Warum Holz im Bürobau vorne dabei sein muss," Zuschnitt 61, 3, 2016

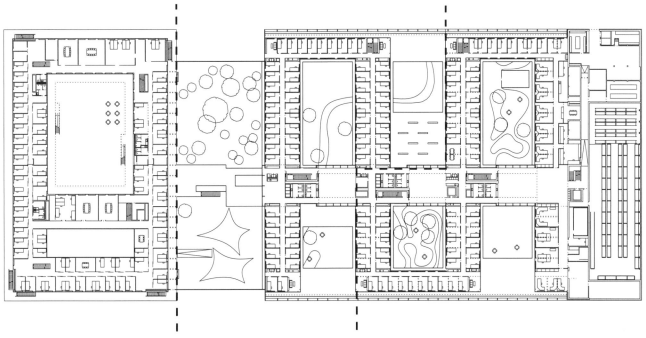

Floor plans, scale 1:1000

The 25 Principles of Building Biology

Building site

1	Building site without natural or artificial disturbances
2	Residential buildings away from sources of emissions and noise
3	Decentralized, low-density developments with sufficient green space
4	Personalized and family-oriented housing close to nature
5	Causing no negative social consequences

Building materials and noise control

6	Natural and authentic building materials
7	Neutral or pleasant smell without releasing harmful substances
8	Use of building materials with low radioactivity
9	Noise and vibration control based on human needs

Indoor climate

10	Natural regulation of indoor air humidity using humidity-buffering materials
11	Low total moisture content of new construction that dries out quickly
12	Well-balanced ratio of heat insulation and heat storage capacity
13	Optimal indoor air and surface temperatures
14	Good indoor air quality through natural air exchange
15	Radiant heat for heating
16	Not significantly changing the natural background radiation and atmospheric electricity
17	Preventing exposure to electromagnetic fields or radio-frequency radiation
18	Minimizing exposure to fungi, bacteria, dust, and allergens

Interior design

19	Considering harmonic measures, proportions, and shapes
20	Natural light, lighting, and color conditions
21	Applying physiological and ergonomic findings to interior and furniture design

The environment, energy, and water

22	Minimizing energy consumption and using as much renewable energy as possible
23	Building materials preferably from the region without exploiting scarce resources
24	Causing no environmental problems
25	Best possible drinking water quality

The 25 Principles of Building Biology reflect the basic tenets of building biology. They are intended as a design guide and as a checklist for holistic assessments. The projects presented in this book are therefore evaluated according to these principles. The assessments look at each principle and whether it was applied to a given project, that is, whether it is applicable (+) or not (-). A neutral (0) score was given if a principle was not explicitly applied, but without having any negative consequences, or the principle falls within the user's control.

New Building
Institute of Building Biology + Sustainability IBN

− 0 +

Repair of irregularities
Preservation of existing building
Expansion of green space
Local craftsmanship
Neighborly coexistence

Wood-frame construction, no adhesives
Wood fiber insulation boards
Cellulose insulation
Clay boards, clay/lime plaster
Acoustic ceiling, ceiling with crushed
limestone and natural fiberboards

Untreated or oiled natural surfaces
Vapor-permeable construction
Clay paints inside, silicate paints outside
Natural insulation material
Controlled air intake and exhaust with humidity
regulation and heat recovery
Radiant heat
Exterior RF shielding with stainless steel mesh
Shielded, halogen-free electrical wiring
Demagnetization of steel reinforcement

Preservation of existing curved building
Proportions according to the golden ratio
Maximum use of daylight, flicker of artificial
lighting reduced as much as possible
Natural colors, ergonomic workplace equipment

Photovoltaic (PV) system
Primary pellet furnace, green power
Regional, abundant, renewable materials
Recyclable building materials
Stainless steel pipes
Decentralized hot water system
Rainwater use

Half-Timbered House

− 0 +

Preservation of village
structure
Local craftsmanship

Wood/clay half-timbered
frame
Reed insulation boards
Clay/lime insulating plaster

Untreated natural surfaces
Vapor-permeable con-
struction
Natural insulation material
Radiant heat

Historical and modern
proportions
Maximum use of daylight
Natural colors

KfW Efficiency House
"Heritage", condensing gas boiler
Wood stove, regional building
materials
Preservation of existing
building, copper pipes
Descaling system

Old Peat Barn

− 0 +

Development interlaced
with green spaces
Individual work model
Local craftsmanship
Labor contributed by clients

Wood-frame construction
Wood fiber insulation boards
crushed foam glass
Clay/lime plaster
Crushed stone

Untreated natural surfaces
Vapor-permeable con-
struction
Natural insulation material
Radiant heat
Thermal mass of clay

Maximum use of daylight
Natural colors

Log wood boiler, solar
thermal system
Wood from the client's
own forest
Preservation of existing
building
Stainless steel pipes

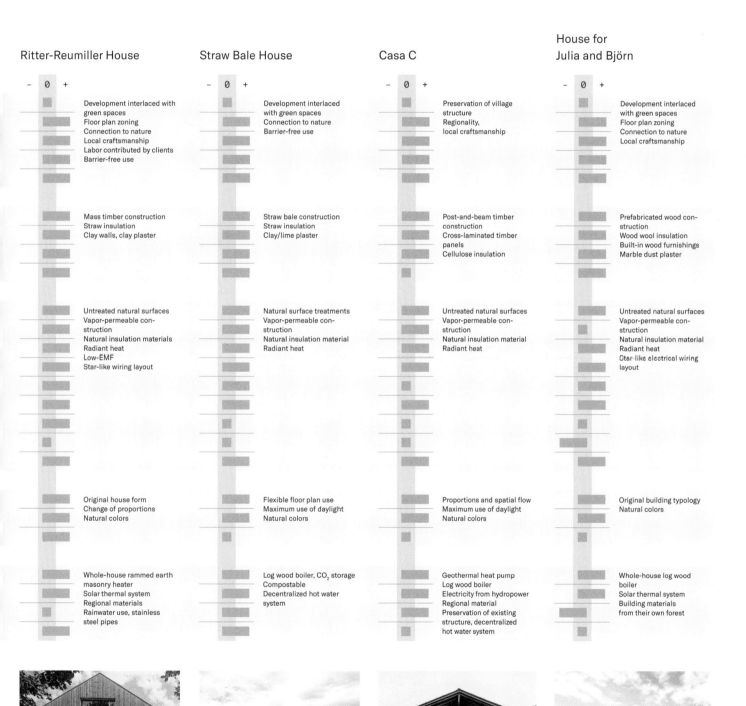

Ritter-Reumiller House

− 0 +

Development interlaced with green spaces
Floor plan zoning
Connection to nature
Local craftsmanship
Labor contributed by clients
Barrier-free use

Mass timber construction
Straw insulation
Clay walls, clay plaster

Untreated natural surfaces
Vapor-permeable construction
Natural insulation materials
Radiant heat
Low-EMF
Star-like wiring layout

Original house form
Change of proportions
Natural colors

Whole-house rammed earth masonry heater
Solar thermal system
Regional materials
Rainwater use, stainless steel pipes

Straw Bale House

− 0 +

Development interlaced with green spaces
Connection to nature
Barrier-free use

Straw bale construction
Straw insulation
Clay/lime plaster

Natural surface treatments
Vapor-permeable construction
Natural insulation material
Radiant heat

Flexible floor plan use
Maximum use of daylight
Natural colors

Log wood boiler, CO_2 storage
Compostable
Decentralized hot water system

Casa C

− 0 +

Preservation of village structure
Regionality,
local craftsmanship

Post-and-beam timber construction
Cross-laminated timber panels
Cellulose insulation

Untreated natural surfaces
Vapor-permeable construction
Natural insulation material
Radiant heat

Proportions and spatial flow
Maximum use of daylight
Natural colors

Geothermal heat pump
Log wood boiler
Electricity from hydropower
Regional material
Preservation of existing structure, decentralized hot water system

House for Julia and Björn

− 0 +

Development interlaced with green spaces
Floor plan zoning
Connection to nature
Local craftsmanship

Prefabricated wood construction
Wood wool insulation
Built-in wood furnishings
Marble dust plaster

Untreated natural surfaces
Vapor-permeable construction
Natural insulation material
Radiant heat
Star-like electrical wiring layout

Original building typology
Natural colors

Whole-house log wood boiler
Solar thermal system
Building materials from their own forest

The 25 Principles of Building Biology

The House of Wood

| − | 0 | + |

Development interlaced with green spaces
Connection to nature

Mass timber construction
Cross-laminated timber panels
Wood fiber and foam glass insulation
Built-in wood furnishings

Untreated surfaces
Vapor-permeable construction
Natural insulation material
Radiant heat
Star-like electrical wiring layout

Original building typology
Natural colors

Geothermal heat pump
PV system, renewable, recycled materials
Rainwater collection

Maison Marly

| − | 0 | + |

Suburban development interlaced with green spaces
Design suitable for family use

Mass timber construction
Cross-laminated timber panels
Wood fiber insulation boards
Impact sound insulation

Natural surface treatments
Vapor-permeable construction
Natural insulation materials
Controlled ventilation system with heat recovery
Radiant heat

An interplay of proportions and perceptions

Wood fireplace
Passive house
CO_2 storage
Green electricity
Decentralized hot water system

Haussicht Design House

| − | 0 | + |

Development interlaced with green spaces
Floor plan zoning
Connection to nature
Suitable for barrier-free use

Wood panel construction
Wood chip insulation
Mineral-based plaster and colors
Nontoxic materials

Untreated natural surfaces
Vapor-permeable construction
Natural insulation material
Indoor air quality measurements
Controlled ventilation with heat recovery
Radiant heat
Shielded electrical wiring
RF shielding gypsum boards

Flowing, natural forms
LED, flicker-free
Natural hues

Air-to-water heat pump
Solar thermal system
PV system
CO2 storage, no waste
Rainwater seepage

De Potgieter School

| − | 0 | + |

Revitalization of historic property
Minimization of disturbances
Connection to nature through gardens
Neighborly coexistence

Reuse of lumber from existing structure
Wood fiber and cellulose insulation
Clay plaster, linoleum
Acoustic ceilings

Untreated natural surfaces
Vapor-permeable construction
Natural insulation material
Controlled ventilation with heat recovery
Radiant heat, star-like electrical wiring layout

Material-specific use of materials
Proportions of pre-existing building
Maximum use of daylight

Gas/air-source heat pump
PV system
Abundant, renewable, recyclable materials
Stainless steel pipes
Rainwater collection

Friedensschule School Annex

– 0 +

Development interlaced
with green spaces
Individual working model
Local craftsmanship
Labor contributed by client

Wood-frame construction
Wood fiber insulation boards
Crushed foam glass
Crushed stone
Lime/clay plaster

Untreated natural surfaces
Vapor-permeable
construction
Natural insulation material
Radiant heat
Thermal mass of clay

Maximum use of daylight
Natural colors

Log wood boiler
Solar thermal system
Wood from the
client's own forest
Preservation of existing
building
Stainless steel pipes

RHS Peter Buckley Learning Centre

– 0 +

Green space
Connection to nature
Barrier-free

Wood-frame construction
Cellulose insulation
Natural paints, linoleum
Acoustic ceilings

Untreated natural surfaces
Vapor-permeable
construction
Natural insulation material
Radiant heat

Psychological effect of wood
Maximum use of daylight
Natural colors

Upgrade of exisiting
heating system
Regional, ecologically
certified building materials
Decentralized hot water
system

Ecolino Daycare Center

– 0 +

Development interlaced
with green spaces
Connection to nature
Free of disturbances
Barrier-free

Wood-frame construction
Wood fiber, calcium silicate
Hemp insulation, clay plaster
Nontoxic building materials
Acoustic ceilings

Silicate paints
Vapor-permeable con-
struction
Natural insulation material
Controlled ventilation
with heat recovery
Manual ventilation strategy
Radiant heat
Demand switches
No wireless networks/devices

Suitable for children
Material-specific installation
Maximum use of daylight
Natural colors

PV system
Local district heating
Wood chips
Abundant, renewable
materials
Stainless steel pipes
Constructed wetland

Pollenfeld Daycare Center

– 0 +

Development interlaced
with green spaces
Connection to nature
Barrier-free

Mass timber construction
Cross-laminated
timber panels
Wood fiber insulation
Clay plaster, linoleum
Acoustic ceilings

Untreated natural surfaces
Vapor-permeable
construction
Natural insulation material
Cross ventilation
Radiant heat
No wireless devices/
networks

Suitable for children
Material-specific use
Maximum use of daylight
Natural colors

Local district heating
Wood chips, abundant
Renewable materials
Decentralized hot water
supply

Herbafarm

− 0 +

Embedded in nature
Organic operation

Wood-frame construction
Cellulose boards
Perlite, reed board insulation
Natural paints

Natural surface treatments
Vapor-permeable
construction
Natural insulation material
Cross ventilation
Electrical wiring kept away
from sleeping areas
No wireless devices/networks

Maximum use of daylight
Natural colors

Passive solar gains
Renewable,
regional materials
Stainless steel pipes
Rainwater collection

Hörger Biohotel

− 0 +

Preservation of village
structure
Connection to garden
Organic operation

Mass timber construction
Cross-laminated
timber panels
Wood fiber
Cellulose insulation
Sound-insulated boxes

Untreated natural surfaces
Vapor-permeable
construction
Natural insulation material
Decentralized ventilation
system
Radiant heat
Star-like electrical
wiring layout
No wireless devices/networks

Physiological effects
of stone pine
Maximum use of daylight
Natural colors

Local heating district
Biomass, PV system
Regional, renewable
materials
Stainless steel pipes
Rainwater seepage

Almrefugio

− 0 +

Preservation of barn
Regional craftsmanship
Barrier-free

Quarry stone wall
Wood roof structure
Heavy timber construction
Wood fiber insulation
Lime plaster, silicate paints
Partition wall
Impact sound insulation

Untreated natural surfaces
Vapor-permeable
construction
Natural insulation (partially)
Radiant heat

Proportions of existing
structure
Lighting concept (LED)
Natural colors

PV system
Existing oil furnace
Renewable, regional,
recycled materials

Casa Salute

− 0 +

Free of disturbances
Area interlaced
with green spaces
Connection to nature
Building biology consultation

Mass timber construction
Mass timber wall
Wood fiber insulation
Clay plaster
Acoustic ceiling

Untreated natural surfaces
Vapor-permeable
construction
Natural insulation material
Decentralized ventilation
system
Radiant heat
Wireless light switches
Halogen-free cables
Layer of brick on reinforced
concrete slab
Shielding curtain
No wireless devices/networks

Natural, ergonomic shapes
Stone pine wood
Maximum use of daylight
Natural colors

Hybrid PV system and
heat pump
Abundant
Renewable materials
Copper pipes
Rainwater collection

Artis
Commercial Building

–	0	+	
			Urban mixed-use development
			Microclimate due to green roof
			Employee-friendly
			Wood engineering construction
			Mass timber panels
			CLT, wood fiber
			Cellulose insulation
			Clay plaster
			Noise barrier wall
			Untreated natural surfaces
			Vapor-permeable construction
			Natural insulation material
			Controlled air intake and exhaust with heat recovery
			Radiant heat
			Internal transparency (space/work)
			Maximum use of daylight
			Natural colors
			Condensing solid fuel boiler
			Waste wood from the company's production
			PV system
			Naturally abundant Renewable materials

Omicron Campus

–	0	+	
			Connection to nature
			Gardens, Employee-friendly design of spaces
			Barrier-free
			Nontoxic building materials
			Wood facade
			Lay interior furnishings (floors/walls/ceilings)
			Wood fiber insulation
			Acoustic ceilings
			Individualized use of space
			Untreated natural surfaces
			Vapor-permeable construction
			Natural insulation material
			Controlled air intake and exhaust with heat recovery
			Radiant heating and cooling
			Low-RF wireless applications
			Meeting areas close to nature
			Maximum use of daylight, LED
			Ergonomic workplace equipment
			Geothermal heat pump with heat exchanger
			PV system
			Certified, regional, renewable materials

Photo credits

Project/photos

New Building of the Institute of Building Biology
+ Sustainability IBN
Institut für Baubiologie + Nachhaltigkeit IBN, pp. 37–47;
Maximilian Mutzhas, p. 47 bottom left

Haingraben Half-Timbered House
Stefan Marquardt, pp. 50–55

Residential Building and Workshop in an Old Peat Barn
Malte Fuchs, pp. 56–59, 61;
Ziegert | Roswag | Seiler Architekten Ingenieure, S. 60;
Stephanie und Emmanuel Heringer, S. 56

Ritter-Reumiller House
Christian Grass, pp. 62, 63, 65 right, 67; Bruno Klomfar, p. 64;
Ingomar Reumiller, p. 65 left; Roswitha Natter, p. 66

Straw Bale House
Adolf Bereuter, pp. 68–73

Casa C
José Hevia, pp. 74–79

House for Julia and Björn
Adolf Bereuter, pp. 48, 80–85

The House of Wood
Erich Spahn, pp. 86–91

Maison Marly
Schnepp Renou, pp. 92–97, 166

Haussicht Design House
Jonas Kuhn, pp. 98–103

De Potgieter School
Daniel Höwekamp, pp. 104–109

The Friedensschule School and Fire Department Annex
Christoph Bijok, pp. 110–115

RHS Peter Buckley Learning Centre
Joakim Boren, pp. 116–121

Ecolino Daycare Center
Florian Schöllhorn, pp. 122–127

Pollenfeld Daycare Center
Erich Spahn, pp. 128–133

Herbafarm
eds-architecture, pp. 134–137

Hörger Biohotel Tafernwirtschaft
Sebastian Schels, pp. 138–141

Almrefugio
Erich Spahn, pp. 142–147

Casa Salute
Meraner & Hauser, pp. 148–153

Artis Commercial Building
Daniela Friebel, pp. 1154–159;
Ziegert | Roswag | Seiler Architekten Ingenieure , p. 156

Omicron Campus
Bruno Klomfar, pp. 160–162, 164–165; Stefan Mori, p. 163

The ground and floor plans were made available to us by the
architects of the various projects.

Acknowledgments

Acknowledgments

The support of the Institute of Building Biology + Sustainability IBN in Rosenheim was invaluable. My special thanks and appreciation go to Winfried Schneider, the managing director of the IBN, for his technical support and to his team at the Building Biology Consulting Office at the Institute in Rosenheim. Furthermore, I am deeply indebted to the Institute for allowing me to use their teaching contents. My thanks also go to all authors of the course modules of the Building Biology Correspondence Course IBN, in particular, Winfried Schneider and the founder of the correspondence course, Prof. Dr. Anton Schneider (died in 2015). Additionally, I am indebted to all project architects, coworkers, and photographers who made their works available and were on hand with help and advice for me. I am also grateful to all the people who were there for me with their advice and encouragement on my journey to write this book, to my family for their support, and to Birkhäuser Verlag for making the publication of this book a reality.

Disclaimer

All contents of this book have been carefully researched and reviewed by the author. However, no warranty is assumed for the accuracy, adequacy, or timeliness of the information provided. The contents of the online version of the Building Biology Correspondence Course up to and including 2017 have been taken into account. Any subsequent changes are beyond the control of the author; the author therefore does not assume any liability. The book contains links to third-party websites; the author bears no responsibility for their contents and therefore does not assume any liability. For the contents of the websites, the relevant operators bear the exclusive responsibility.

Imprint

Concept: Nurgül Ece
Subject matter expert: Winfried Schneider
Translation: Katharina Gustavs
Editor: Raymond Peat
Project coordination: Alexander Felix, Regina Herr, Lisa Schulze
Production: Heike Strempel
Design: Peter Dieter, Dorothea Talhof (www.formalin.de)

Paper: 120 g/m² Amber Graphic
Print: Beltz Bad Langensalza GmbH
Lithography: [bildpunkt] Druckvorstufen GmbH

Library of Congress Cataloging-in-Publication data
A CIP catalog record for this book has been applied for at the Library of Congress.
Bibliographic information of the German National Library.
The German National Library lists this publication in the Deutsche Nationalbibliografie; detailed bibliographic information is available online at www.dnb.de.

Printed on acid-free paper produced of chlorine-free pulp.
TCF ∞
Printed in Germany

This publication is also available as an e-book (ISBN PDF 978-3-0356-1040-6) and also has been published in a German language edition (ISBN 978-3-0356-1179-3).

© 2018 Birkhäuser Verlag GmbH, Basel
P.O. Box 44, 4009 Basel, Switzerland
Subsidiary company of Walter de Gruyter GmbH, Berlin/Boston

ISBN 978-3-0356-1183-0

9 8 7 6 5 4 3 2 1

www.birkhauser.com